DURHAM VILLAGES

Durham
Villages

HARRY THOMPSON

ROBERT HALE · LONDON

© *Harry Thompson 1976*
First published in Great Britain 1976

ISBN 0 7091 5825 4

Robert Hale Limited
Clerkenwell House
Clerkenwell Green
London EC1 0HT

To my father—six years too late

PRINTED IN GREAT BRITAIN BY
CLARKE, DOBLE & BRENDON LTD.
PLYMOUTH

Contents

Illustrations

PICTURE CREDITS

All pictures are by Bill Hardie, except 9, 12, 45, 46, 47 and 55
which are reproduced by courtesy of the Newcastle Chronicle and
Journal Ltd., and 25 and 34 which are reproduced by courtesy of
the Planning Department, Durham City Council.

I

Monkton and its Magic

THE village of Monkton, with which this story of the villages of Durham begins, was a small rural outlet on the fringe of Jarrow which itself was (and is) on the banks of the Tyne. In my childhood Monkton was a place of magic, eternally surprising, yet as affectionately familiar as scuffed old boots. On Saturdays when you were free, and on the endless holidays when the sun always shone, and life seemed to be suspended in the stillness of mid-afternoon, Monkton beckoned with an infinity of indulgence.

There was Seymour's farm and at the back the cows grazed in the shadow of the brooding gigantic slag heap—of which very much more anon. Opposite there was Handyside's farm where one picnicked on Bank Holidays. There was Hoyle's House with its enticing pear-trees in the front garden, and Mr Hoyle with his club foot and stout stick to swish at you, although, truth to tell, the dangerous pastime of pinching the pears had results which were far from delectable. The pears were hard; they invariably caused a pain in the stomach. Better when Mr Hoyle put broken glass on his wall and that stopped the marauders altogether.

At the back of the Lord Nelson Inn there was the golf course, and here the magic became intense, for at the first tee, almost in the foothills of the slagheap, was Bede's Well, while at the side of the course were the playing fields of Monkton Home, which was a place for mentally retarded young men. In those less socially conscious days we approached the home warily fearful, despite our bravado, of what might befall us. It was known euphemistically as the Dooley Boys Homes, this being a derivation, I believe, of the Indian word *Deolali*, a place where the heat was so overpowering that people who lived there feared for their reason. Beyond the Home and the golf course, fringing the village, were the lakes of Hebburn, made by man, it is true, but places for tiddlers and sticklebacks, and swamps where the flag iris and the marigold thrived.

The Well, in reality a simple spring in the ground, was protected by an iron grille. We were all versed in its alleged miraculous powers, for St Bede, who of course had lived in the monastery at Jarrow in the seventh century, was said in local legend to have passed that way and taken his refreshment. If you had faith the water was said to cure your ailments. Once, in 1740, a score of local children had all their illnesses cured. We, credulous and sceptical at the same time, ready to believe, ready to sneer, often tested the powers of the waters with—I regret to say—the most disappointing results. The ice-cold water, though, was a good if temporary alleviation for raging toothache. We used to skirt the village day after cloudless day rather in the manner of Just William and his gang. There was the garden with the bronze eagle on a plinth, the little church of the Venerable Bede, and then, veering away from the presence of the slagheap, past the Methodist chapel and the insanitary houses, there was the Dene which had steep grassy banks, a mass of trees, and rabbits, weasels, stoats, a hare or two and a family of badgers.

Nearby, across a farm road and through a path flanking a few council houses was the shop that sold home-made ginger beer at one penny a bottle. It was so volatile that you could make the corks hit the ceiling, and the fish and chips at the shop next door were the most delicious that were ever made anywhere.

We had a trio of cricket teams. It needed an excursion of more than a mile to watch the Venerable Bede team play beside the railway line, and to witness (on one momentous occasion) the squashing of the only cricket ball by a passing train. But the Monkton team itself played in a grassy bowl not far from the Dene, and middle-class young men who were members of the Junior Imperial League disported themselves on a bumpy field where it was imperative to afford the luxury of a matting wicket otherwise life itself (not to mention limb) would be endangered.

An unexceptional village, I suppose. No great historical happening had ever disturbed the placid nature of its ways. No battle had been fought here; there had been no plague or pestilence. Monkton was mentioned, it is true, in the Boldon Book, which was a survey of the estates of the See of Durham drawn up by order of Bishop Pudsey in 1183, but the reference is of the most fleeting.

Yet there was always plenty to do in Monkton. But why, you may well ask, was a slag heap situated amid such rural delights?

Well, the heap, in fact, was a vast, oblong mountain of solid rubble, the waste of decades of activity at the Jarrow Steel Works, a couple of miles away. The works closed in the Depression but one of my first recollections is lying in a dark bedroom which suddenly was illuminated by a bright red light which would glow momentarily and then quickly die away. This was the tipping of the molten lava from the top of the heap. The glow had illuminated Monkton for decades.

But now, with the works closed, the heap was brooding and idle, but it was a place full of mystery and fascination with caves and gulleys, down which, on sodden winter days, the waters would gush. I remember an excursion to the top at five in the morning, the better to see an eclipse of the sun. Monkton, without the accompanying presence of the heap, would be unthinkable.

At least so we always supposed—when we thought of it at all, that is. But going back there, assessing in the cold disenchanted light of adult life how Monkton is today, one discovers a disconcerting, indeed, in retrospect, a terrible fact. The slag heap is gone.

Monkton, indeed, is very different. The placid, enclosed life has been succeeded, it seems to me, by a bustling urbanization which is much worse and which is accompanied by distressing signs of dereliction. The heap is gone to pave the motorways of England, I dare say, and this, from an environment point of view should be an advantage but somehow it is not.

It has been succeeded, at the moment at least, by a considerable acreage of rubble at approximate eye level. The golf course is gone, too, and in its place are houses and buses and a whole new indeterminate life. The lakes, the flag iris, the marsh marigold have disappeared, buried as well under bricks and concrete, and though Bede's Well survives, it is now pathetically vandalized. The pure waters which at least cured my aching teeth are dank now and covered in slime. They would do you an exceedingly ill service were you to imbibe them now.

The Monkton Home, now known as the Monkton Hospital, is sprucer than I ever knew it, and the bronze eagle is still on its plinth. The pear trees still grow profusely and in one of the farms where we picknicked there is a park for caravans.

The little church of the Venerable Bede, boarded, its windows shattered and its little garden overgrown, has a Sold notice posted outside. The Methodist chapel survives, but the insanitary houses (I am sure quite rightly) are gone. The Dene is tamed; it has path-

ways and bridges, and many more luxuriant trees. Now there are
no cricket teams. The Junior Imperials and their matting wicket
are long gone and there are council houses in their place, and I
walked in vain round a maze of crescents and avenues looking for
the bowl where Monkton played.

I suppose you should not go back, at least not equipped with
the deep, detailed and unfair knowledge of childhood. So, as I sat
in the bar of the Lord Nelson Inn talking to a man who grew leeks
and deploring change—all change, in the large, airy, generalized way
one does in pubs—a young man from the Monkton Hospital came
in and doffed his cap just as they used to in the days gone by.
And then I got a silly illusion, just for a second or two, that I
really had not come back at all.

2

Jewel among Villages

WESTOE VILLAGE is an anachronism. There is no reason why
a village should survive within the centre of an industrial town,
perched almost apologetically on the side of a main road within
listening and sniffing distance of the noise and the racket, and
within sight (at its extremity) of the bingo parlour, the betting
shop, the supermarket and the doleful queue for bread. (The
queue was a purely temporary phenomenon, there being, on my
succession of visits, a bakers' strike.)

Westoe, *circa* 1974, just before Christmas, wears a sad and ex-
pectant air. It is suffocated with the cars of the intrusive students
from the Marine College nearby; someone has scrawled "Spock
OK" on the walls of what Pevsner describes as "one of its higher
and showier houses". Some typical urban clutter—a TV repair
van, a window cleaner's ladder, and a passing student of exem-
plary scruffiness—somehow disturb the early Victorian rectitude
of another house, smaller, more distinguished, of which Pevsner
is complimentary. He calls it "nice".

If Westoe, therefore, exudes an aura of refined pessimism this
is scarcely surprising because, I suppose, its great days are done
and it must wonder how the multitude of planners are proposing
that it should continue its days.

Westoe Village, a sort of annexe to the larger Westoe District
of South Shields, has an entrance from the A19; it needs a
straight left turn through a gateway as the car points towards
Sunderland and the vision is ahead of you. Dugdale in 1819
described this vista as "consisting chiefly of one respectable
street inhabited by successful maritime adventurers who have
retired". Nowadays, though the names Manor House, Chapel
House and Derwent Lodge remain, the adventurers have gone,
presumably to their ocean valhallas and there is a nursing home,
a rest home, a residential hotel, while Westoe Hall, a vast Victor-

ian pile, once owned by the town's main shipbuilders, the Red-
heads, is inhabited by the Education Department.

Westoe has its assiduous historian, the late Miss Amy Flagg
whose lovingly inscribed two volumes were deposited in 1966 in
the South Shields public library. One of these volumes, indeed,
traces the occupants of each house in the village's heyday, and
though she may regret the passing of the Greens and the Wallises,
the Heaths and the Andersons, she betrays little sentiment, hers
being a sternly factual approach. She tells us that the original
name almost certainly was Wivestoua, which in Anglo-Saxon
means Ladies Land. But, though she is assiduous, there is very
little cohesive history she can write about Westoe village. She
quotes one account, written at the end of the eighteenth century
when the ancient smithy still stood. Then there were four or five
houses on the right side of the village. Just past the second house
was the village pump at the entrance of what was then the bridle
path to Harton. At the top of the village, just as the rough road
narrowly insinuated itself into the broader environs of the main
Westoe district, there was the high pond and a beautiful view
(then) of Tynemouth Priory across open fields. There was also a
low pond with ducks, and it was in this vicinity, seemingly, that
the lady archers disported themselves.

Miss Flagg and others recall childhood memories of walking
over the fields in the dying years of the nineteenth century to do
the shopping for mother in King Street, adding much gratuitous
(and here irrelevant) information about the idyllic prices then
appertaining, and the late hour to which the shops stayed open.
It remains only to be added that it is a hard slog on concrete to
King Street nowadays, and the view from the head of the village,
far from encompassing the Priory over the fields, takes in only a
pleasant suburban picture of bricks and mortar with—it is
admitted—more trees than is customary.

Westoe village, truth to tell, reached its zenith of respectability,
not to say prestige, as a dormitory and cocoon for shipowners and
shipbuilders and other wealthy local families in the late nineteenth
and early twentieth centuries.

It was nearly ideal for their purpose, being close to their place
of business and, with its white railings fringing the rural pathways, its grassy swards and tall regiments of sycamores, presenting
the atmosphere and the enviability that their position demanded.
It was certainly the ambition of the businessman of substance to

live in 'the village', and was seen as the accolade success had conferred upon them.

It would be felicitous indeed to suppose that the time of the village's greatest animation might have been frozen and that, to this day, the carriages might have wheeled out of the gateway bound for shipyard and river and foundry—felicitous and not really very practical since time goes on—and time, meaning the last decade or two, has not been on the side of the village. Much of the life has gone out of it, though, of course, private residents remain. There is now an institutional air: it is a pity there is not a shop or a pub, but this latter amenity, if it had atmosphere, would attract more cars driven by outsiders than ever the students can aspire to.

Now, with the recent reorganization of local government all over Britain, and the consequent proliferation of experts in planning, the fate of Westoe village is discussed in many committees, and many highly paid professionals give it their consideration. A Conservation Order covers the village so that nothing may be pulled down or altered without the complexities of various planning acts being invoked. Indeed no paint may be applied to a building unless it is in line with a colour code which has the approval of the Civic Trust.

What perplexes the planners, of course, is how Westoe village can retain what life it still possesses, and conceivably begin a process of rejuvenation.

How to chase away the cars of the students without plastering the village with double yellow lines, but much more importantly, how to bring more people to live there in family units? Can the huge houses be split up appropriately, or would the cost of this be so prohibitive that the only people able to afford it would prefer to continue to live in their split-level executive bungalows far away from the town centre?

Failing this, is it not better to allow the village to be increasingly (even completely) taken over by institutions rather than see a descent into seediness?

This is the dilemma of Westoe village and it is beyond the wildest dreams of the Barnes and the Wallises and all those merchant adventurers who came home from the seas to its green swards, its prestige and its quietude.

Cleadon, which one reaches two or three miles further south along the A19, does not have the protection of the enclosed Westoe situation. The main road runs through its heart; the pleasant village

street is stuffed with cars, for this is executive dormitory territory;
long streets of splendid houses and an exclusive estate or two,
and a couple of pleasant pubs, 'The Britannia' and 'The Cottage'.
Cleadon, though (and this is not nearly so obvious), has its hill
and rolling common land, its history of secret passages and ghosts.
There are distinguished residences of some antiquity: Cleadon
Tower and Cleadon House. There was also (and this fell neatly between the last two) the Cleadon Gap which gave the village a
fitful notoriety.

You came upon the gap after the Tower which is just behind
the war memorial. Then there is the handsome village post office
followed by the chemist and the hair stylist—and then there was
the Gap. The story—or the mystery—of the Gap deserves a little
attention because it is at once simple, sad and significant.

Not so long ago four Georgian cottages stood there, splendid
little specimens built about 1740, and though they had no outside
sanitation, the pensioners who largely lived in the cottages were
certainly happy there and kept them, so it is said, "like little
palaces". The cottagers, it need hardly be said, added to the
picturesqueness of the street.

One day, though, rumours began to filter into the village, the
substance of which was that the cottages were to be demolished
because land at their back had been acquired by a development company to build an estate of rather pricey houses. It was ironical, and
the subject of some bitter humour at the time, that these houses
were to be "Georgian".

The prospect of the demolition of the cottages was denied—
several times. It was at the same time said that a public health
inspector—a chief public health inspector no less—had categorized
these cottages as "slums". To this one of the outraged pensioners
replied that no such person had ever been in her house, anyway, for
thirty-five years at the very least.

Then, one day the occupants received a letter from an estate
agent saying that their homes had been "acquired" and indeed
were to come down because an access road to the new estate was
needed. The villagers, perhaps belatedly, stirred themselves to
form the Cleadon Village Action Committee of which their leader,
Miss Rosalind Kersh, was magnificently a fighter. A deputation to
London followed, but nothing, it seemed, could halt the trend of
events which seemed to be inexorable.

So the cottages came down. The development company provided
alternative accommodation for the inhabitants, but the plea that

perhaps only two of the cottages need to be demolished to make way for the road was rejected.

So, for quite a while, there was a glaring gap, but now there is a new house, and only a small gap as an entrance to the 'Georgian' estate behind and it is all a little sad, and I doubt if anyone truly believes that the village street has been improved although, truth to tell, with its clutter of styles, and sense of being submerged by the car, its charm was mostly destroyed before the story of the Gap began.

Of course this is not a black and white episode. The developers properly rehoused the pensioners who were on record as being happy in their new abodes and it is no sensible planning philosophy to maintain decrepit examples of the past. But could the cottages not have been saved—or at least might not two of the four have been retained? If the village had been protected by a Conservation Order as is Westoe and Whitburn (whose story will presently be told) it is at least possible that the furore aroused by Cleadon Gap might never have occurred. Conceivably the Gap would never have been there at all.

However, true Georgiana still pervades the village, for next door is Cleadon House, a most delectable example built by John Dagnia in 1738. There is a fine wrought-iron staircase, a room used by Charles Dickens, and the present owner, Mrs Crowell, has fantails disporting themselves on the lawn. Seeing these gracious birds just outside the conservatory on a cloudless summer day and with the façade of the house as a handsome backcloth brings a sense of excitement to anyone whose imagination is spurred by scenes from the past. However, you are pretty soon jerked back unceremoniously to the present. Traffic thunders by continuously outside, and the whereabouts of Cleadon House, should you be a stranger in these parts, is easily pinpointed. It is almost exactly opposite the supermarket.

Still, Cleadon House is a glorious place, redolent of the atmosphere of its times and like all pure Georgian buildings, particularly the smaller sort, so precisely right, that the rooms, even now, seem none too large, and the marvellous wide doorways, so fashioned to allow the crinolines to sweep through, impress one as being utilitarian even in the 1970s. No trouble about moving furniture, even of the most bulky sort. You simply shoot it straight from one room to another.

Charles Dickens, visiting one of the Abbs family, who owned the house for several generations, heard the curious story of an

B

earlier tragedy in the family, and how the dining-room had been prepared for a pre-wedding party when the bride declared the whole thing off.

The bridegroom thereupon decreed that the room should forever stay as it was on that fated day: the dining table in all its magnificence. At the beginning his edict was obeyed, but "forever" is a long time. The room and the story behind it caused immense interest in the village and the local folk came to gaze through the windows. To prevent this the windows were first painted black and then bricked up. You will find the story, though altered out of recognition, in the saga of Miss Havisham, the mad bride in *Great Expectations*.

At the Towers at the opposite end of the street you are swept straightaway into a far more violent past. No mention here of gracious Georgian ladies, of parties and assemblies. Instead an odd little tale is told, one of the oddest and most sinister I have heard around the villages of Durham. When the present owner, Mrs Margaret Brigham and her late husband were putting the house to rights they decided on the demolition of an interior wall in the dining-room, which extended from the old original fireplace. When they pulled down this wall, so that they could put a window in the outer wall, they discovered the skeleton of a cat, without doubt an original Tudor cat, put there when the house was built in 1490. It was the fashion in those days thus to bury a cat alive to preserve the house from witchcraft. Mrs Brigham buried the Tudor cat in her garden where it still lies, now side by side with the remains of a cousin of the 1970s.

The Towers has a ghost, of course, whose crunching footsteps used to be heard deliberately treading the gravel path in the garden. A previous owner, annoyed and maybe even frightened by this, had the gravel replaced by paving stones and nowadays the ghost's occasional intrusions are less noisesome. But, yes, Mrs Brigham and her husband had certainly heard the ghost, unless it was a freak of the wind.

The Towers had a priest's hole which is now a cupboard; the fascinating original Tudor oven remains, and just in front of the spit in the kitchen there is an odd sort of protuberance on the stone floor. It was from this spot that a passage (secret or otherwise) was launched and continued under the road and in the general direction of the Britannia Inn. There are a few romantic stories as to the reason for the passage, but all, most likely, are apocryphal. In the rebellious, not to say licentious days, when Cleadon Towers was young, a way of escape was always needed from intruders, doubly necessary here since the Towers probably then stood almost alone, outstanding amid the hovels of the labourers. So much, though, is conjecture, since the owners of the Towers have never felt it necessary to commit their experiences to print.

Memories of the Chambers family, owners of the Towers from the end of the fifteenth century for several generations, would have been particularly rewarding. Summers, the historian, tells of members of this family being excommunicated by the powerful Bishop of Durham for refusing to grind their corn in the Bishop's Mill. Thus they were denied burial in consecrated ground and were buried in their stackyard at the north-west of the house. In 1927 when excavations for sand were taking place, the remains of five adults were discovered and it was assumed that they were those of the excommunicated people. The whole story, incidentally, was seen as confirmation that the house existed in pre-Reformation times. Henry VIII's rupture with the Pope took place in 1531, and afterwards the power of the Bishops was severely curtailed. Excommunication for such a paltry offence would have been inconceivable at any later time.

The original Tower, set slightly apart from the house, was pulled down by a previous owner, Richard Pemberton, in 1780, but this apart, the original structure is marvellously preserved, the walls, in some places being six feet thick. Real vandalism seems to have occurred only once. A local shipowner, briefly the owner of the Towers in the 1840s, pulled out the circular stone staircase.

Despite all this antiquity, the real history of the village is scanty indeed. Cleadon had been linked with Whitburn in the Boldon Buke in 1183, and for centuries the two villages were classed as joint holdings within the Manor of Chester and belonging to the Prince Bishops of Durham. But there is no continuous thread of history by which the story of the villages can be told. No political disturbance seems to have touched Cleadon, though trouble, of a military sort, was perilously close during the Civil War.

During this period Newcastle was held for Charles I, and in consequence the coal traffic from the Tyne was stopped. This was a vital matter for the South, so Parliamentary troops were stationed at Sunderland to protect the coal trade from the Wear. In 1644 and 1645 several skirmishes took place at Boldon Hill and Hylton. No doubt Cleadon—only a couple of miles away—felt the reverberations of these struggles.

Otherwise—nothing murderous. In the late eighteenth and early

nineteenth century the village was on the turnpike road and the
stage coach departed from the Ship Inn (now demolished) each day
at 8.30 a.m. and 6.30 p.m. John Wesley preached at the village
chapel, and though idealistic people nowadays deplore the passing
of the village pond (and of so many village ponds) it is a fact that
usually (and especially on hot summer days) it exuded a decidedly
rich aroma. The whole situation was a little less satisfactory than
the rose-tinted memory of older people would have us believe.

Across the old turnpike road (now the busy A19 previously
referred to), past more pleasant houses up a winding pathway and
Cleadon Hill is upon us. This is an elevated stretch of common
or farm land from which you may walk to the sea. It is rolling
country, bleak in midwinter, slightly more welcoming in summer.
Stand in its centre as the east wind blows and the clouds scud
across the skyline, and there is a sense of isolation every bit as
forbidding as that presumably felt by the inhabitants of the
Towers long ago when the silence of the night was broken by
thudding on the front door and hectoring cries outside.

An odd tale concerns Cleadon Hill and the creation on the side
of a limestone cliff nearby of the figure of a white horse. John
Gibbon, a Victorian farmer and stockbreeder, was in the habit of
bringing ponies from the New Forest for taming and sale. Once
when the master was away one of his labourers, William Johnson,
rode a pony which took fright and plunged over the cliff and was
killed. The children of the labourer drew a crude figure of a horse
to mark the spot and the legend was born. Soldiers encamped on
the hill during the 1914–18 war painted the horse, and Scout
parties continued the tradition. There was a period when the image
of the horse became disreputable and even somewhat mottled, but,
I am glad to say, when last seen it was in pristine condition.

From Cleadon it is only a moment by car, but half an hour,
much more rewardingly, by foot to Whitburn, Cleadon's cousin,
and a veritable jewel among the villages of Durham. I plead guilty
to bias. I cannot be truly objective where Whitburn is concerned.
Images of its cricket ground are enshrined in memories of childhood, though it took a bus journey and a good hour's walk to get
there. I have gone back repeatedly since to watch cricket, to walk
on the cliff top in the direction of Roker, or simply prowl in Front
Street, where, behind the green and the war memorial, are the
houses I covet so much: Olde House, Orchard House, Cross House
and best of all, maybe, Laburnum House, magnificent all in their
early Victorian pleasance. This part of the village is superb as you

look across to the tall, commanding avenue of sycamores, the grassy banks and on a higher promontory, Whitburn House, with its remarkable folly. I have seen nowhere in the North-east of England that I would rather live. Just here—not even anywhere else in this most delectable of villages. Just here the atmosphere is right. There may be a passing regret for the increase in cars, and the noise of the occasional lorry, but there is the comfortable reflection that since Whitburn sits snugly between main roads, the A19 and the coast road both in their differing ways going from South Shields to Sunderland, there is no practical reason why the traffic should ever rend the village apart and destroy its character.

Like Westoe, a Conservation Order now protects Whitburn, and this of course covers the village's main building, Whitburn Hall, in front of which the cricket team disport themselves. But Whitburn Hall is falling down. Conservation Order or not, permission will have to be given soon enough to the company who nowadays owns Whitburn Hall to demolish the place and build the modern development which is presumably its intention. Whitburn Hall is no architectural gem, being a rambling amalgam of a number of styles with concrete excrescences which are positively unsightly.

But its demise will finally cut the ties of the village with the Hedworth Williamson family. This will be a pity, for village and family have grown together, as it were.

The association began in 1719 when Sir William Williamson, the fourth Baronet bought the Hall, married into the Hedworth family and so founded the dynasty. The family took up residence in the Hall in 1735—and lived there until 1946. They seem always to have been a picturesque family: the stories that emerge about them infallibly have a glamorous—almost a rakish tinge. They were of the village yet, of course, so much apart. That same fourth baronet with whom their story begins, encamped with a posse at Gateshead in 1743 to prevent the Scots marching south. A later baronet—I think it was the seventh—fought a duel with his political opponent during the General Election of 1832—but no one was hurt. The same gentleman caused a whole sheep to be roasted on the village green to celebrate the coming-of-age of his son. Beer, liberally supplied from his own brewery (suggested to have been established at the gates of the Hall) lent a Bacchanalian air to the proceedings. The following Sunday baronet and son attended divine service and listened to a sermon on the evils of drink.

The sixth baronet—he lived from 1751 to 1810—trained two Derby winners, Ditto the winner in 1803 and Pan in 1808, largely on the sands at Whitburn. One of his successors—evidently a very considerable eccentric—criss-crossed the lawn of the Hall with a maze of high walls, the curious purpose being to exclude the sea breezes. All that the walls kept out was the sun from the main drawing-room. The walls were pulled down when the curious baronet was in London attending to Parliamentary business.

Nowadays, the Hall stands silent. Spurious-looking Grecian figures, twelve feet high, with baskets of fruit improbably on their heads, guard the frontage, but the back is broken and vandalized.

The church in Whitburn is unexceptionally of the thirteenth century, though the upper portion of the tower is later. The flat-topped gravestones with which the churchyard abounds, were used in the seventeenth century to serve beer and bread to the poor when, as was the local fashion, these had been bequeathed by some affluent notability. In later years, the church has achieved a certain local fame for the quality of its music. This was not always the case. During the long incumbency of the Rev. Thomas Baker—he was Rector for fifty-six years until 1866—the church acquired a barrel organ which was installed in the chancel. The difficulty was that there was a certain unpredictability about this organ which would sometimes continue its music long after the singing had ceased. On occasions such as this the barrel organ had to be carried out of the chancel—still merrily bellowing forth—so that the service could proceed. Apparently the organ was in due course shipped to Australia, but the ship sank *en route*.

Whitburn House, which stands high above the village street in all its mock Tudor flamboyance has a remarkable folly to the rear of the house. This is a stone church window in the English Gothic style acquired by Mr Thomas Barnes, owner of Whitburn House, in the mid-nineteenth century, from St John's Church, Newcastle where extensive alterations and tidying up were then proceeding. The window, from the ruins of some ancillary building at the church is known as St John's Temple. The fact that it is there at all is a fair indication of the arrogance and eccentricity of Mr Barnes—Squire Barnes as he adored being referred to. He was a wealthy coal-owner with decided ideas of his own consequence, and this fact led to a delectable—and significant—confrontation with the village. In front of Whitburn House are banks of green. Upon this grass since the Middle Ages it had been the habit of the local women to spread out their washing to dry.

Squire Barnes thought this demeaning; in fact he seriously doubted their legal right to do so. He began by roundly condemning the practice and then he forbade it. When his injunction was ignored he sent out a servant to pour dirty water over the drying clothes. Then the villagers acted. They took Squire Barnes to court and received an award for damages. He refused to pay but was forced to do so by a ruling in the Queen's Bench Division in 1873 when the rights of the villagers were clearly outlined. No one, I regret to say, dries the washing outside Whitburn House today.

The sea breezes previously referred to, or the 'sea fret', the local name for the creeping mist which insinuates itself and shrouds half the village a few occasions every year, has been known to hold up play on that otherwise delightful cricket ground. The pitch is bigger now, but in earlier years it had an intimacy not usually seen, including a massive tree well inside the boundary line. You got four runs if you hit the tree.

There used to be a small but healthy fishing industry from the village: ten boats each using a crew of three fished—among other things to provide a regular supply of turbot for the London market. Because of the structure of the coastline and the perilous rocks close by, wreckages were frequent, particularly before the advent of radar. Thus it was an appropriate enough place for early experiments in the use of rockets to fire lifesaving equipment to inaccessible places. The last time the equipment was used was in 1937 and nowadays, of course, the ships keep well away from the coast. But a hundred lives were saved by this method in one forty-year period in the nineteenth century. Many of them, one supposes, were from the tiny ships that engaged in the local seaborne trade, for Whitburn was utterly isolated by land. As an example of this isolation, coal for the village, mined at Wearmouth Colliery, was brought by sea, and trundled ashore at The Bents, a part of the coastline that is relatively free of rocks.

Nowadays there are new housing estates to the east, north and west of the village. To the south of the village the buttercup meadow has been replaced by a splendid park, and pubs like 'The Jolly Sailors' have a cosmopolitan air about them. Northward the old colliery was closed in that period when Lord Robens wielded his axe on the British coal industry, and a little further north still equidistant, almost, between Whitburn Village and South Shields, the colliery at Marsden is likewise silent.

There is nothing much to Marsden, I suppose, except a row or two of colliery dwellings, the Grotto and the remarkable rocks on the beach.

'The Grotto' is, in fact, a very successful inn hollowed out of solid cliff face. In 1782 a character known as Jack the Blaster finding the cost of living in South Shields too expensive for his taste, took up residence in a series of caves hereabouts. Later a former gamekeeper of the Marquess of Londonderry named Peter Allen kept the first inn here. Life seems to have been somewhat precarious with waves occasionally breaking over the bar, once almost carrying away the Allen children.

Now owned by a brewery combine, the whole area is very spruce. There are 124 steps (or you can go by lift) from the cliff top to the beach and to the Fishnet, Cavern and Beachcomber bars. Down here sea fishermen cast their lines from the edge of the surf, and you can wonder—if you have a tithe of romantic imagination—at the remarkable rock formation just a few yards offshore. How did this solid island of rock remain and all else be worn away?

Even odder, though, is the phenomenon a couple of hundred yards to the north where a thick spire of rock half the height of the cliff face (and only a yard or two from it) rises in the sands. Of the numerous wonders in this unpretentious corner of Durham the rocks at Marsden, in my judgement, are certainly the most remarkable.

3

Old and New

THE simple traveller who tries to get to the old village at Washington is confronted with many problems. If he proceeds via Newcastle there is the motorway to be negotiated and then the veritable maze of new roads of Washington New Town which, in their seeming eccentricity (the signposts have numbers, not names) conspire only to confuse.

If (as I did) he approaches from Boldon the tentacles of the New Town similarly stretch out in a stranglehold, and though signposting on this side is infinitely more intelligent, there is still a feeling that, like Alice, you have gone to the other side of the Looking Glass.

Alternatively, as you spin down side-roads to junctions and feeder roads and dead ends, seeing the Old Hall and the church beckoning—so near yet so utterly far away—you feel as bewildered as when, for example, you are caught in a modern maze of one-way streets in a town that is foreign to you. In Bournemouth and Colchester I have ploughed helplessly onwards seeming to get further and further away from hotels I was seeking to enter. Thus it is at Washington when the mission is much more simple—at least at the beginning: just to take a glass of beer and a sandwich at the Washington Arms (no sandwich: it was Saturday) to explore the Old Hall, the church and the pottery, and to assess, maybe, how old things are married to those rampantly new.

But there are moments of intense diversion long before this judgement may be applied. On Boldon Hill Pevsner talks of the ruined red brick building, remnant of a Victorian smoking house, the theory, the mythology or whatever having it that the place was created because some virago (she can have been nothing less) so bullied her husband (he was a local shipbuilder) and nagged him about his smoking habits that (poor old codger) he had to retreat to this haven on the hill, there to smoke his pipe in peace.

A nice story which, I feel, would deserve to be true, even if it was not.

In any event the red ruin, being remote from the road-way and protected by prolonged and muddy fields, denied me the chance of casting an eye upon it. I would have appreciated this and will make the journey on a drier occasion since, I am told, the story used to be recounted with relish by a generation or two of nagging wives as illustrating the justice of some for-bidding action of their own. What is not recorded is whether the reactions of the husbands were as spineless as that of the shipbuilder.

Boldon itself, East and West, has its cricket ground on the very edge of Sunderland (where the Hardys, Harold and Donald, father and son, distinguished themselves for so many years). A couple of miles away there is the church on the verge of the hill. That is Boldon, straddling the A184: a nice early Victorian house or two, 'The Grey Horse', 'The Black Bull' and the Boldon Flats. There is also Boldon Colliery, an associated village of quite differ-ent atmosphere and pretensions in which the ethos of pitmatic Durham is clearly defined.

Boldon Flats is a sunken common-like stretch of land which sits somewhat tenuously on colliery workings which from time to time subside. When I was a child and the winters were harder—or seem to have been so—the Flats used to flood and freeze, and skating parties made a pretty sight. Even at night a congregation of car headlights illuminated the scene. Nowadays the Flats are drained so, of course, the skating is no more and they are used, so far as I can judge, by cows and by a few reluctantly exercised and yapping dogs.

But sterling deeds did happen in the slightly more distant past. They had horse racing there at the beginning of the twentieth century, and the Flats were also used often enough for testing the early aeroplanes. The story is told of the visit (it must have been about 1911–12) of Madame Franc, the intrepid pilot of a bi-plane of the period. The lady lurched crazily, while either land-ing or taking off one day. In doing so she hit a flagstaff, killed a small boy, and very seriously injured herself. When she recovered sufficiently to be pushed about in a wheel chair she told of her exploits before packed houses at the Sunderland Empire Theatre. Madame Franc, who now is something of a folk hero in the minds of older men and women, seems to have been a sight more fortun-ate than most. Many of the planes experimenting in this territory earlier in this period flew only a few yards and then turned over or crashed into hedges. More than one pilot was killed.

St Nicholas Church, nice and unremarkably thirteenth century except for a lovely brief spire, repays the searcher for delightful architectural detail. If you look assiduously you will find, in the stone, a fourteenth-century priest commemorated thus: his feet rest on a pair of beavers, which unite in one head. Query: Did he keep beavers or was his calling somehow associated with them? Otherwise it is a mystery. And so, after the mischances I have described, and past the Sunderland Airport and the melancholy (because recently closed) Usworth Colliery, to Washington Old Village. It used to be the unassuming, countrified centre for a group of collieries categorized by letters of the alphabet. Now every colliery has gone and the old village sits (uneasily I think) beside the vast and increasing colossus of the New Town. This, aside from its town centre and shopping centres, is being created as a complex of villages of which the old village will be one.

Still, if you probe and look beneath the unpromising surface, which Washington especially on a rainy morning can undoubtedly present, excitement and not a little disquiet bubbles. Where is the old village of Washington going? Why is it so difficult to explain (as the potters in the old smithy would ask) the drop in the hosts of American pilgrims, and why even the livelihood of the indigenous villagers is now endangered?

I absorb these attitudes and also those of the planners who, it seems to me, faced with an impossible conflict of views have been both civilized and accommodating. Their contention, somewhat loosely translated, is that when they took over the old village it was cascading rapidly downhill, and the tawdry nature of the main street would seem to encourage that contention. The place was festooned with overhead wires and since a main north-south road link passed directly through the village, there was eternal persecution from juggernauts, and what remained of the old village was permanently shrouded in the vile fumes of diesel.

So, they put the wires underground, tidied up the village green and the pond in which, in more forthright days, witches were immersed for their own good. They attended to sundry other environmental matters such as cleaning up the churchyard, utilizing some of the outbuildings of the Washington Glebe Pit beside the vicarage as an adventure playground, and would have incurred the wrath of the villagers not at all if only they had not (as part of a much grander New Town design built the Eastern Highway.

This had the pleasant effect of re-routing the juggernauts so that now the road along the village street, past the Cross Keys and the Old Hall *en route* to Fatfield, the Wear and the journey south, is occasionally almost deserted.

I tested this as I moved out of Washington in search of further surprise at Penshaw Monument and Hylton Castle, and in two miles or so to the river I saw not another vehicle. This, having the effect of making the village quieter, also means that it is now cocooned, rather like a habitation on the very edge of a peninsula. Takings of the businesses in the main street have declined, in some cases drastically, and Bob King, who now runs King Pottery in the old smithy, is not taking kindly to the resultant isolation. He came from the artistic colony at St Ives in 1971 (a disciple of the great Bernard Leech) and makes anything from beer mugs for local hotels to free ranging experiments in what he describes as an extension of the medieval tradition. His lamp bases in functional sculpture (you make a rough sketch but, really, you cannot tie yourself down too rigidly; you've got to let the clay take over he explains) are expensive but, it seems to me, weirdly beautiful. Bob King and his assistant are a little nostalgic for the days when busloads of Americans and Italians drew up outside and, though they only had a grotesque fifteen minutes to 'do' the Old Hall next door, they generally managed to pop into the pottery. This type of passing trade was vanishing, for fewer and fewer conducted tours of foreigners breathlessly passing from London, via Stratford-on-Avon to Edinburgh, did the detour to see the home of the ancestors of George Washington.

"For one thing," Bob curtly observed, "they can't find the place. You've got to be pretty determined to get here at all." True enough, though I am bound to add that Mrs Margaret Douglass, the remarkable custodian of the Washington Old Hall, did not subscribe to the views of Bob King and saw no diminution, really, in her American visitors. The book they sign at any rate seemed to indicate that individually the Americans and the Italians and, surprisingly, the Japanese were still assiduous and (I was told) knowledgeable about the past. The remarkable fact though about the old Hall is not that it is so spruce and well cared for (it is, after all, the property nowadays of the National Trust) but that it exists at all.

It is a small manor house originally built in the twelfth century and it was here that William de Hertburn, the first known ancestor of George Washington, had his home. He arrived in 1183 though it is not known whether he built the house or it was here before him.

As was the fashion, the family assumed the name of the place that now belonged to them and became de Wessyngton. Four generations later an ancestor, John, married an heiress and moved to Kendal, and thereafter to Warton in north Lancashire. It is eighteen generations precisely from the move of this branch of the de Wessyngtons westward that George Washington (a fourth-generation American) was born in Virginia.

All this and much more besides is known to the great majority of the modern American visitors to Washington, Co. Durham, whose knowledge of the complexities of the family tree are decidedly more detailed than that possessed by the passing Englishman who will begin, often enough, on the assumption that George Washington was born here—and be mightily disappointed when it is pointed out that the connection is more remote and less romantic than that.

Disappointment is increased when it becomes known that the Washington Hall extant is a mere (though pleasant enough) seventeenth-century structure, though with some small aspects of the original hall embedded in its fabric. It is fortunate, indeed, that even this building still persists. After several generations of neglect it was parcelled up into tenements in the 1920s and finally condemned as unfit for human habitation in 1936. Thus it was within days of demolition when local opinion marshalled by Fred Hill, local headmaster and real saviour of Washington, stepped in, formed a committee and the hall, in effect, was saved.

The present condition of the hall owes a deep indebtedness to affluent Americans who not only provided much of the original money for its resuscitation, but also gave furniture, panelling, busts of George Washington and much else besides. Under the management of the National Trust the Hall is kept in pristine condition, and if the mind recoils slightly at the spectacle of plastic roasts revolving on the mechanical spits, and plastic representations of a seventeenth-century lady and gentleman on either side of the fireplace, then perhaps this is being unnecessarily critical.

If I have conveyed the impression that Washington Old Village is somewhat down-at-heel and anxious about the future then this is certainly true. As the New Town grows (to its zenith of an 80,000 population by the 1990s) it may be that it will be swallowed up completely and lose what character it still possesess. But by then, at least, the old people who complain that they "know nobody now" and who look somewhat askance at the invasion of the young in the New Town villages on their doorstep—will have gone and with them, maybe, the conflict.

There is, though, an aspect of old Washington more of interest to the social historian than any remote and lateral association with George Washington, and this is its deep involvement with the early digging for coal in Co. Durham. This was the village's mind and heart. It existed for the people scattered around the flat fields and hamlets, living and dying in all those Washington pits from A to J and other undesignated hollowings in the ground which were known as bell pits. They began digging coal here as early as 1600 and the last shaft was sunk as late as 1925. And how in the past the miners have died for their living! There were seventeen disasters between 1766 and 1908, for example, and all were explosions, mostly followed by entombments. The catalogue of disaster is not really well documented, though, and you look in vain for any expression of social resentment at this profligate waste of life. Most of this came later and in other areas of the Durham coalfield. Here there was a more passive acceptance of fate aptly expressed in numerous epitaphs: "George Reed, Overman, Fell Asleep: Alas he never awaked more. But to his home his corpse was borne. He lived happy, thus he died. 'Twas God that took him to the skies."

As I left Washington the winter rain had now ceased and the road down to the river at Fatfield (and thereafter, whichever way I turned into the deep recesses of the Durham coalfield) was deserted. But swinging through Penshaw on the road to Sunderland a remarkable sight meets the eye. It is a sight of which I never tire. As a schoolboy in another part of the county I had its vision eternally on the skyline—a gaunt, blackened version of the Temple of Theseus.

Whichever way you approach Penshaw Monument—for that is what it is—you are conscious of a diminished sense of the wonder which the ruins of ancient Greece bring to your heart. Not only why did they build this colonnaded monster of the hill—but how? The answer is manpower and horespower, both of which were cheap—and there it is, suddenly to your left as you mount the steep road, as great an anachronism in this modern age, as useless and monstrous a depiction of unloveliness as any residue from the industrial revolution.

Still, life would be a little more dull in Durham without Penshaw Monument, erected in memory of John George Lambton, first Earl of Durham, so much a progressive of his day (he died on

28th July 1840) that the local miners christened him Radical Jack. He owned the immense Lambton estates, had an income of £80,000 a year, was a revolutionary Governor General of Canada, and an enlightened landlord of the wide acres of which his monument is fittingly the centrepiece.

Local mythology goes a bit crazy where this edifice is concerned. It was erected, some seriously suggest, because everyone was pleased when Radical Jack reduced their rents. Then he came back from foreign wars, laughed in derision at what they had done, and proclaimed that if this was how they spent their money, the rents could go right back up again. So the monster was left unfinished, minus the projected statue of Jack on its summit.

The mind boggles at all this, especially since the monument was not finished until 1844—four years after Jack's death. In truth it was a pretty spontaneous tribute to a remarkable social figure who combined a libertarian zeal with a proper, indeed extravagant pomp and ceremony. The miners loved both.

The monument is just twice the size of the original Theseus and in the late nineteenth and early twentieth century was an object of wonder—so much so that pilgrimages to the site were made by hundreds of people each summer weekend. In those days you could climb to the top and feast on the considerable panorama before you. Then the inevitable happened. A boy fell from the top and died, climbing the monument was banned, the crowds drifted away, and quite forbidding fences were put up which stop all but the vandals. Nowadays both the National Trust and, I believe, the N.C.B. are considering the fate of Penshaw Monument. I only hope they do not pull it down. It is in such classical bad taste that it deserves to be retained.

Hereabout the villages of Durham are in defence against the encroachments of the town of Sunderland, the more so since so many of the collieries have been closed down, tight corporate communities have been dissolving, and village life, as the miners and their families understood it, has been difficult, if not impossible to maintain. Shiney Row, Philadelphia, Hylton, both North and South, East Herrington, New Herrington, Offerton—and many more. It is often impossible to know where one ends and the next begins, or which has been swallowed by Sunderland. The spread of council housing has been intense; it is, all in all, an area typical of so many in industrial Britain and improbable (to say the least) as a situation for a castle. But castle there is—and it is mystifyingly difficult to locate.

Yet I drove on, the rain returning, and enquired on the side of a busy road the whereabouts of Hylton Castle. There was a ready enough response. My first informant gave me explicit directions: turn left, drive for a mile, turn right—and there you are. There I was, too, bang in the middle of the streets, avenues and crescents of the Hylton Castle Estate.

So where, I enquired again, was Hylton Castle? That was easy, said the lady emerging from the supermarket: straight down the main road for three hundred yards, a slight incline to the left— and you couldn't miss it. Nor could you—if you wanted the Hylton Castle Arms. But there at least the comedy ended. Just beyond the pub this massive estate ends, and there is a green field with Hylton Castle in its centre. This is the perfect castellated stone box, the sort of castle a child would draw for its school teacher. It is perfect —and dead.

Hylton Castle is fifteenth century and has a most melancholy ghost, the Cauld (or Cowed) Lad who is both headless and forlorn. He sings of the miseries brought on the Hylton family because of his death. He was a stable boy who failed because of lassitude to saddle his master's horse in time. For this he was murdered with a hayfork.

Certainly the ghostly prophecies that the Hylton estate would be broken up among many owners have come to pass. Certainly owls nested in the castle walls, and without the ministrations of Government and the affection of antiquarians it would certainly have fallen down.

People on the Hylton Castle Estate take a proprietary but sadly neglectful interest in the castle on their doorstep and the visitors, such as they are, are nearly all experts and of an archaeological turn of mind. Once, though, Hylton Castle stood out among a group of hamlets and small villages. Now, almost as difficult to find as Washington Old Village, it is utterly lost in suburbia.

The slag heap at Monkton

A shady avenue in Westoe

Cleadon House, a lovely example of Georgian building

Whitburn Hall, now falling down

The King Pottery in the
old smithy in Washington
Old Village

In the village of Whitburn

Washington Old Hall, where the first known ancestor of George Washington lived

Hylton Castle, utterly lost in suburbia

The unfinished Penshaw Monument, erected to the memory of the first Earl of Durham

Herbert Cooper, a retired miner who has made his name as a painter

A street scene in Easington

A picture from the past: a miner, nowadays, goes home clean

Golden sands at Seaham

A busy summer in Crimdon

4

Colliery Villages

The Victoria History of County Durham, edited by William Page and published in 1907, says this: "Intoxication is a painfully common vice among the colliers especially at weekends, while the language and behaviour of the crowds (of miners) at football and bowling matches too often recall the habits of their medieval ancestors. . . ."

Daniel Defoe in his *Tour through the Whole Island of Great Britain,* has this to say of a pit explosion he seems to have witnessed at Chester le Street in 1724: "A new coal pit being dug or digging when (the foul air) blew up like a thousand barrels of powder—with such a terrible noise as made the very earth tremble for miles around and terrified the whole country.

"There were near three score poor people lost their lives in the pit, and one or two of them, as we are told, who were at the bottom of the shaft, were blown quite out, even though they were sixty fathoms deep, and were found dead upon the ground."

The *Durham Chronicle* of the period comments thus of the disaster at Seaham Colliery in 1880 when 164 men and boys were killed. "A very touching incident was made known. Among those who preferred to stay in the Hutton seam on Wednesday while his workmates were making efforts to get out, was a young man named Dixon whose father had been previously rescued. Dixon's reason for sticking to the spot—was that his putter boy had been injured. When the explorers got near to him they besought him to endeavour to come to them, but to their earnest solicitations he simply answered that he preferred to remain by his injured lad. This morning Mr Bailes while exploring the No. 3 Hutton seam found young George Dixon lying dead with his arm around the neck of the lad. . . ."

At the same pit during the same disaster a message was scrawled on a board by entombed miners, subsequently discovered, and

c

preserved: "The Lord has been with us and we are ready for Heaven. Ric Cole, ½ past 2 o'clock, Thursday."

Then, a little later: "Bless the Lord we have had a jolly prayer meeting, every man ready for glory. Praise the Lord, Sign R. Cole."

J. B. Thompson, a coal-hewer and pamphleteer, writing in 1843: "In the present year the masters of several collieries have made a reduction of no less than 20% (in wages). . . . Then there is the arbitrary system of plunder in the shape of fines by the infliction of which it is nothing strange to hear of several pitmen, after a hard day's work, coming to bank in debt. . . . There are families actually in a state of starvation—there are men who have not had a morsel of food in their houses for days together, and who have been obliged to beg for a few turnips for the children to break their fast. If we allow this year to pass over, the next year we will be in a worse condition than the handloom weavers are at present, that is living on three or four shillings a week. How long can a collier live on skilley and such like food? My friends, think of these things for a moment. We are worse treated than the Children of Israel who were compelled to make bricks without straw. Our masters bind burdens upon our backs grievous to be borne. . . ."

The Marquess of Londonderry, owner of virtually all he surveyed in the coal village of Seaham, was so irritated with the way local tradespeople were helping striking miners in 1844 that he wrote the famous Seaham letter: "Lord Londonderry again warns all shopkeepers in his town of Seaham that if they still give credit to pitmen who hold off work and continue in the Union, such men will be marked by his agents and overmen, and will never be employed in his collieries again. . . . The shopkeepers may be assured that they will never have any custom or dealings with them from Lord Londonderry's large concerns that he can in any manner prevent. If credit is so improperly and fatally given to his unreasonable pitmen thereby prolonging the injurious strike, it is his firm intention to carry back all the outlay of his concerns— even to Newcastle.

"Because it is neither fair, just or equitable that the resident traders in his own town should combine and assist the infatuated workmen in prolonging their own miseries by continuing an insane, and an unjust and senseless warfare against their proprietors and masters. . . ."

Sidney Webb, in his book *The Story of the Durham Miners*, describes the astonishing system whereby the miner was bound to his employer: "On Binding Day the Bond was hurriedly read out by the manager in the open air before a crowd of men of all grades—hewers, putters, firemen, enginemen, pony drivers, onsetters, banksmen—few of whom could follow what he was reading or even hear the words. Then and there the men had to put their marks—very few could sign their names—to the document which was to bind them in involuntary servitude for a year. Hiring money or Binding Money was paid to them; in the middle of the eighteenth century only sixpence; one hundred years later only a few shillings. At some collieries the diabolically ingenious system was introduced of setting up among the crowd of men a rush to sign, by offering £1 to the one who got there first, ten shillings to the second, five shillings to the third, and only 2s. 6d. each to all the others. . . ."

Richard Fynes in *The Miners of Northumberland and Durham*: ". . . A few men who were unionists at heart banded themselves together at Thornley, Trimdon and Monkwearmouth and thus formed the nucleus of the present Durham Miners Association, which was formally called into existence in the month of November, 1869. . . ."

There is a mass of literature about the Durham miners; so much to read, indeed, that you could go on for a year or more and not exhaust the drama. For drama, almost totally, it is. Much of the writing is statistical and is concerned with the rise in personal productivity, with technical data about how the early pits were sunk, and about tonnage then, and all the years and decades until now.

But the real story of the Durham miners and their pits and their families is a personal one. And the wonder, as it emerges, is that the type of people should have been so idiosyncratic, so brave, so independent, just as though there had been some divine ordinance in their choice. Somehow, if one is excessively fanciful, one can imagine the right people being directed where the challenge was fiercest. Alternatively, and this is really the nub of the matter, the people who were required to sink the early pits in Durham, to grapple with nature to make them a success and with all the appalling conflict and disaster, were properly of the calibre to ensure that there would be no final failure. They have been compared, both in personal characteristics and what they had to do, with the covered wagoners who moved from East to West in America in the early nineteenth century: pioneers all.

Looking at all this in 1975, a curious story unfolds. Now, as we shall see, a great majority of the pits are closed. The small village adventure whereby a few men founded a small community, sunk a small pit, and (in aggregation with all the others) created a great substance, is dead. Now, by and large, the Durham mining community survives and prospers in larger groups, in pits where the seams are higher, the productivity by comparison immense, the miner efficient in the use of complex machines, incomparably safer (disasters are thankfully rare).

Now the small pits are mostly silent and the small mining villages, so brave and fascinating in the lives led there and the stories unfolded, have lost the reasons for their existence. Some of these villages are disappearing. It is a sad phenomenon of the '70s for the planners to decide when such a village has no future life, and when this happens pit cottages are allowed to crumble and die, and the few people who remain (usually old and set in their ways) are gently channelled into a more salubrious atmosphere not far away. Then the remnants of the pit cottages are bulldozed down and (there are already several signs of this) the weeds and grasses encroach and the district begins the journey back to the rural quietude from which a century ago or more, it sprang.

By contrast, in the coastal strip of Durham where the pits are big and prosperous and growing even bigger, dynamic factory techniques take over, and areas exude optimism. Miners come in by bus from all the dead areas in the hinterland, and there is a holiday in everybody's heart. It is boom time in Horden and Easington and Blackhall and Westoe and Wearmouth and Dawdon, and a closing of the days at Langley Park. And at Quebec and Quaking Houses where the pits have long been silent, there is a long remembering and a concern for other matters.

This is the way it is. But it is permissible, relevant and even crucial to concern oneself with the way it was to see how the past conditions the present. This is vital, for wherever you go in the pit villages of Durham, and however young and untainted by the past the miner and his family may appear to be, you discover that the history of the family broods and conditions almost all responses. This is not necessarily good or bad but it is so. How then in 1975 is the Durham coalfield really behaving?

There is still, to a degree that outsiders would find difficult to comprehend, this deep awareness of the past, of the days in the nineteenth and early twentieth century when death was common and injustice passionately proclaimed. There is still a harking back, almost masochistically, to the days when every village had its pit, when the pithead dominated the scene, and when so many large families (up to twenty children) were held together by the love and character of the mother. These families were proud, religious, puritanical, ranting, hard-drinking, obsessed by the pit. Indeed there is no conception by outsiders what the miners endured, how they lived. There is still a consciousness of all this; still vociferous in the old and sometimes silent in the young, but it remains bright and untarnished.

The good neighbourliness you find everywhere may be less imperative now, but there are a dozen good reasons why it should remain and why the village communities, even where they now have no village pit, should continue tight, clannish, sometimes suspicious of outsiders, but inviolate.

I think any introductory chapter of the story of the pit villages of Durham as they are in the middle 1970s should recognize this. But it would likewise be both misleading and silly to ignore the brutal and licentious past because it conditions in a crucial way what happens to the present.

Nowhere in my not inconsiderable experience have I found people so forthright, so friendly, so sensitive to criticism, so hungry for education, so willing to drink deeply, so aware of their own sad and noble history, so proud and defiant as the Durham pitman and his family. Speaking of them as they are now you must remember that they have been participants, either willing or otherwise, in a social and industrial revolution. Since Nationalization Day in 1947, 114 pits in Durham County alone have been closed. They have been pits of every description, but they have always been unprofitable, sometimes small and isolated. In most cases the seams of coal have simply given out or have proved to be surpassingly difficult to quarry.

These pits have sometimes been named after people: Alma, Emma, Randolph, Clara; after places with strange sounding names: Esh, Roddymoor, Watergate(!) and Hole-in-the-Wall. They have had names redolent of vanished, easier going, more rural days: Rose Cottage Drift, Washington Glebe and Stargate. They have, finally, had the names of the places where the coal was dug: Kibblesworth, Whitburn, Hetton, Pelton, Crookhall, and very many more. All have disappeared, usually in the sensible name of rationalization, but not always for this reason.

It is a nice point how many of the 114 would have survived if the British people, and more especially successive British Governments had foreseen the inflation in oil prices from the Middle East, and had therefore more endearingly cherished the miner and the pit.

If 114 pits have disappeared, then it follows that villages and hamlets have undergone severe traumas. Some, candidly, are utterly different places in which one-time miners work at new, modern, light industrial factories. It is both sad and ironic that some of these ex-miners, rendered redundant and who had therefore embarked on new careers making small, clean, consumer goods, should be redundant again as hard times descend upon their new chosen industry. And this at a time when the mining industry (in Durham as elsewhere) cries out for experienced men. There are signs, indeed, of a full circle here, of miners departing, for example, in the mid-'60s to make ball-bearings, returning to hew coal.

From some villages the miners commute *en masse* and by Coal Board bus to the big pits on the Durham coast. And in these big coastal villages previously mentioned where the huge pits push out ever further under the North Sea, the spirit is often one of high optimism. For now coal is king again, and the miners are its loyal, but always intractable subjects.

Their jobs, of course, are signally different, but life underground remains hard. If you are at the coalface, for example, operating—and I quote—a "shearer fitted with nucleonic steering", and the pit is Dawdon which is the largest in Durham, you still have an exhausting, conceivably unhealthy, claustrophobic and highly demanding task. If you are the manager of the self-same pit or one like it where the annual turnover is up to £10m, you have the approximate responsibilities of the managing director of a complex of several factories.

You may be a graduate of the Harvard or the London Business School, youngish, clever, but you may well still, basically, be a pit lad. You will have a modest office, few of the obvious trappings of success, common in other spheres, and you will come to work each day equipped to go down the pit as occasion demands. You will certainly talk to the men unassumingly in their own language not only because this is pit democracy in which you have been reared, but because the miners will tolerate nothing less.

There is now, and has been for years, an egalitarianism about the life of the pit village and divisive factors have either dwindled or disappeared. The social power of the overmen and deputies scarcely exists, nor does the subtle snobbery of the chapel. Indeed the chapels, scenes of such revivalistic fervour, and of such bitter competition one with another, have diminished alarmingly in number. Relatively small villages which had three chapels now have one, or else two, each with only a skeleton congregation. Others have simply fallen down, been pulled down, or are in use bewilderingly as factories or warehouses. Diverse indeed are the uses put to places where once were the pews of the Primitive Methodist (by far the biggest religious influence in pitmatic Durham) and where the Wesleyan preachers thundered.

The pubs flourish, though old-style drunkenness is almost totally absent. To see a man staggering uncontrollably from the drink is an utter rarity as is the Friday or Saturday night fight. There used to be dozens each weekend in the good old days. Nowadays, of course, the beer is weaker, the women accompany the men, and sometimes at least a meal is the first priority with the drink only an accompaniment.

The colliery clubs are munificent places. They have sophistication allied to surpassing luxury. The social life is compounded of hard drinking, the absorbed organization of a variety of hobbies, and entertainment which is of an enviably high standard. At the club the old are treated with generosity and compassion, so many free pints at Christmas as to last the pensioners well into the New Year.

The villages, in a curious way, still remain in isolation from the rest of the regional community. There used to be proper and understandable reasons for this but now, of course, none of these obtain. Most of the Durham pit villages are within thirty minutes drive of Newcastle, and even nearer to Sunderland.

But how do you get to Witton le Wear, or Esh or Metal Bridge? Even though, with intermissions, I have lived in the North-east all my life and have had a fair knowledge of the miner I simply did not know. Nor, when a consensus of NCB and NUM friends urged that I visit Langley Park did I (I am ashamed to say) know where that was either.

Langley Park, indeterminately between Durham and Consett but a mile or two from the main road, is a village of 5,000 people which—at first sight—has a somewhat grim aspect. This grimness which, it turns out, is utterly misleading since the people are warm-hearted and the girls (I was happy to observe) both smart and pretty, first becomes apparent because the brown and grey stone with which everything is constructed scarcely conveys the gayest of welcomes.

There is, in fact, a look of the West Riding about Langley Park, and to arrive in Quebec Street in the centre of the village, as I happened to, on a misty dank day in February makes you feel that some brooding, Brontë-esque tragedy is about to be enacted.

This is all a somewhat feverish fancy, since Langley Park is eminently a practical place with a history which is full of the fascinating folklore of the miners, a present which is (by comparison at least) sturdily prosperous, and a future which is far from predictable.

It also has lots of claims to distinction and at least one philological mystery. Somehow you expect the miners to speak in the 'thee' and 'thou' fashion of north-west Durham where the accent, especially when spoken at speed, is exceedingly difficult even for someone from another part of the region to comprehend. Instead the speech is virtually accentless, only the keenest and most knowledgeable ear detecting the gentler tones and occasional burr of Weardale.

This is because the sinking of the village pit a century or so ago coincided with the closures of many of the lead mines in Weardale. The miners moved to Langley Park changing one form of excavation for another. They brought with them and imposed their speech, and also their sparse, puritanical Primitive Methodist religion. They brought also an atmosphere of a wide open town, and their differences from the rest of the people were heightened by the practice of the indigenous population of referring to them by the places of their origin.

Thus it was Tow Law Bob, Stanhope Bill, Wolsingham Arthur. They were usually hard, patient workers, and their sternness at home—they were often enough the very essence of the working-class Victorian and Edwardian paterfamilias—was not always enlivened by Christian charity. At chapel they could thunder from the pulpit with a homely interpretation of the faith, and the congregation of their fellow workers and families would intervene so that, at times, the tiny place would reverberate with their fervent "Praise the Lords" and "Hallelujahs". Yes, Langley Park in the earliest days of the pit so far as religion was concerned was a Primitive Methodist village, but, as always where you had rigid religion you also had the boozers.

Sometimes when a boozer began the family line, succeeding generations were pillars of the chapel, in more than one instance attaining the ministry. Sometimes, though the reverse side of what is a fascinating field for social exploration is not well documented, the agony and rebellion aroused by too fundamental a Christian approach drove the sons to drink.

Tom Gardner, miner for fifty years, delegate to his union HQ, small, brown-skinned and vital, is also a teetotaller—though not for any religious reasons. His story is typical enough: not that I am suggesting that Langley Park fifty years ago and more was any more drink-sodden than any other mining village.

Every Friday night his father arrived home without his boots, having sold them in the pub after he had poured all his pocket money down his capacious throat. Sometimes he sold his jacket as well, and more than once he sold the house furniture (it had cost £80) to his workmates for a fiver.

Pretty well he would do anything for a drink. One occasion he was knocked down by a motorcyclist and rendered unconscious, the poor driver being unable to avoid him as he staggered along the dark road. The chap pushed him in the side car, drove him home where he was revived, and presented him with half a crown. "For that kind of money," said Gardner senior, "you can take me up the road and have another bash."

Old Gardner would sell his miner's concessionary coal. Once a farmer got two loads for ten bob. And once, when beer was short in the village, he and a friend heard that some was available in a pub a couple of miles away. So they set off in a storm to track the beer down: through the fields, ploughed fields and all, and at the pub they filled a farm bucket three-quarters full and got back with it to Langley Park so that their marras (or workmates) could have a drink.

The boozing went on at weekends, usually, while the kids cowered at home: but again a bit of perspective is needed. If the pubs were full it was maybe only with 100 or 150 chaps, and if you looked for reasons, well, the thin seams in the pit choked the life out of them and invited oblivion. And the pubs were comfortable, whereas a family of eight or nine, or maybe as many as fifteen, overflowed from the bedroom into the dess bed—this bed folded into a cupboard during the day and was let down in early evening to hold perhaps six children lying head to toe. The resultant chaos naturally drove some fathers away to the pub. The tale of Tom Gardner's father had a happy ending. His son was watching a football match, Langley Park versus Stockton it was, a tremendous local occasion. He was behind the goal when a penalty was awarded. "But do you know," he says now, "I never saw it taken. My father had gone away from home on the booze and I was thinking about him while the match was on. Then just as this penalty was about to be taken a woman popped her head over the fence. 'Tom, your father's come home,' she shouted. I forgot all about the penalty and dashed home. There was my father sitting on the fender in the kitchen. He had a Bible in his hand. 'Bonny lad,' he said, 'your Dad'll never touch another drop of beer.'

"And he never did, though that didn't mean he became as bigoted as many a reformed drunkard, even though he joined the Methodists. In fact when he got his pocket money he'd give me half a crown to give to his old drinking pals and tell them to have a drink on him."

Langley Park nestles (there is no other word) at the beginning of the Brownie Valley, and after decades of pollution from the by-products works fish are beginning to return to the river.

Before industrialization, though, this valley and the Deerness valley next to it were alive with game. There was a rule then, enforced by the Earl of Durham who was the major landowner that no man could keep a dog or cat because of poaching, and in the early mining days men would get the sack for refusing to be rid of their pets.

Poaching apart, the miners could when working in concert have a devastating effect on the rural life which was (and is) just on their doorstep. Once when wood and fuel was short the villages unanimously—or so it seemed—decided to raid and cut down the fir trees in the nearby Doctor's Wood. This they proceeded to do under the cover of darkness and over one or two nights. The trees —there would probably be dozens of them—were cut up and stored in the miner's out-houses. Here in due course, but belatedly because they were the very last to know, the police organized systematic raids. Tom Gardner recalls the simple expedient of his family to avoid detection; they packed him off to bed with an apparent illness, placing a large log on each side of him under the bed clothes. Then when the police came and suspiciously eyed the empty outhouse Tom's mother innocently exclaimed, "Oh, do look wherever you like. There's only young Tommy ill in bed upstairs, though." The police accepted this explanation and departed on their ways.

The village had its ash heap: this was where the ash from all the cottage fires was tipped. But it was also the place where good cinders were inadvertently tipped among the ashes. In hard times the children of the miners went to pick the cinders, and Tom Gardner recalls taking turns with his brother to keep a vigil at the heap throughout the night, snuggling among the ashes for warmth, so that they would still be in possession to resume their cinder gathering in the morning. Otherwise, if they had succumbed to the relative comfort of their homes, there were dozens of children ready to take their places.

A hard life? One supposes so, but Tom Gardner remembers it all without bitterness. His memory, as everyone's, is selective, so that, along with his father's escapades he can remember also the love and affection and the astonishing *camaraderie* which permeated the village. Life was tough in the pit, of course, but then it still is, for the colliery is not one of those huge coal factories like they have at the coast. For here you can still lie in a thin seam working a pneumatic pick with your shoulder touching the roof, and maybe there is a couple of inches of water, as well. So, when you emerge, as on occasion you can, wet and slimy, you may wonder why you are so daft as to continue when they're crying out for experienced men at the coast. Other miners, from the massive, drier, profitable pits, tell you you are crazy

But, says Tom Gardner, it's better the devil you know. . . . And the miner, however militant, can be a conservative creature at heart, at any rate in matters of working for a living. His attitude has some logic as well of course. Living and working in Langley Park, he can leave his home, walk to the colliery, do his seven-and-a-quarter-hour shift and be back home all within eight hours.

But what would happen if he turned into a miner commuter? The NCB would take him there and back by bus but it would still be a ten to twelve hour day, and that would be less time for the family, the club, the chapel (a few still take religion into their consideration) the pigeons, the greyhounds, the leeks, the fishing, and even taking the wife out. Against all that the hazard of being soaking wet and slimy is of little account. But situations like this are few enough in the Durham coalfield and getting fewer. There is really no future for the Langley Park Colliery and despite the convenience, little regret it when it becomes too costly to continue. In fact, as I write, news of the impending closure comes through, and the village simply—and fatalistically—prepares for another future.

Langley Park has gained a sort of fame through television. Scenes from a drama of mining life, *Days of Hope*, were shot in Railway Street which is the village's only completely unmodernized row of cottages. I have lived in such a row—albeit in Northumberland, and they are warm, snug, with a vast fireplace in the living

room on which, in different times, the coals were heaped: one
bucketful on the fire, another at the back to be raked easily forward. It was in front of such a fire that the father and sons of the
family bathed, and Railway Street is like that to this day, though
nowadays the houses are usually given to old people. For my conducted tour of Railway Street I had not only Tom Gardner but his
friend Herbert Cooper, a remarkable recently retired miner, tall,
handsome, a black beret on the back of his grey head. Herbert had
a part in this film: you may have seen him. He was a hard-
drinking miner: he had to drink whisky. "Lucozade!" he says in
mock disgust.

They speak in glowing tones of the community in Railway
Street. How the wives would come out to pour the bathwater
down the communal drain which still runs by the side of the
pavement, and how there would be a fight if you slopped the
water into the section of the family next door. They used to put
the bread out on the sills to cool, and though Sid Chaplin, the
Durham miner-author, said that in his village the tramps would
steal the bread and were generally hostile, it was not like this in
Langley Park.

In fact they had a pretty good relationship with the tramping
fraternity who came through the village *en route* to the work-
house at Lanchester. They would sing you a song for a penny, sell
you a rabbit skin for twopence and the skin of a hare for a penny
more. The outside lavatories or 'netties' still stand across the
lane in Railway Street, and these have a profound social significance not only in Langley Park, but everywhere in pitmatic
Durham.

In an area and at a time when privacy was almost impossible
to achieve, the netty was a haven of quietude. Father retreated
there to read his paper; this is not a ribald idea. The families in
Railway Street, as everywhere, were large: the kids tumbled over
each other. Even if they did not, there was baking, washing, iron-
ing, the constant bathing, and the neighbours popping in and out,
the meals at different times because of the shift work. So you
crossed the lane into the netty and you read your paper: Tom
Gardner recalled magic lantern shows in the netty. A girl who became a deputy headmistress in the Midlands, did all her studying
in the netty because there was not a scrap of space for her in the
house. She did it by candlelight in the winter until she could stand
the cold no more. In the summer the light came through a large
ventilation hole, often in the shape of a star, in the door.

It is very quiet in Railway Street now, and the waste ground at the beginning of the street where the handball players became so expert is usually deserted. At the other end is Spion Kop, a district of colliery houses built at the time of the Boer War battle from which its name is taken. Now the houses are 'revived' which in the gobbledygook language of the planners means they have been modernized at great cost—and very nice they look. Then they were the homes of the large families who were "looked down upon", Herbert says, because of the fecund nature of their lives.

One little demon who ruled her family of nineteen children with the aid of a horse whip from the pit is still recalled with a certain affectionate admiration. "But even the farm hind wouldn't live there," says Herbert, searching for some appropriate social analogy, "and he was pretty low."

Facing Railway Street is the old railway which used to run from Durham to Consett Iron Works and is now just a narrow vale and beyond is the spoil heap, as unlovely as these things can be. So is the acreage of waste ground where the by-product plants used to stand. Collectively this shoddy area needs a good going-over but it is pretty low down anyone's priority list.

I said that Herbert Cooper is a remarkable man and so he is. He retired prematurely and suddenly he started to paint. There had been no artistic rumblings in his soul; no agonized frustration. He started, almost, out of social conviction because he believed (and rightly) that so much of the miner's heritage was being lost. "I mean, soon, there'll be nobody who knew the miner's kitchen in the old days with the dess bed down, and Dad in the bath in front of the fire, and mother baking or black-leading the stove."

Nobody would know of the ritual when the butcher called late at night—and nobody, certainly, would be able to describe with any accuracy, the ritual killing of the pig which went on in so many colliery rows in the old days. So he decided to record all these facets of a vanishing life in oils and now he is quite famous. He has had a huge one-man show and four of the best of his works have been in an exhibition in the Tate Gallery. There is a rude, uncompromising vitality about his work which reminds one of Lowry. He is a happy, obsessional painter, a natural actor, too, as those BBC producers discovered, an earnest seeker after knowledge as are so many of his generation, and a bit of an authority, too, on the geological movements which wrought the Brownie and Deerness valleys.

Herbert and Tom were my guides, too, as we moved out of

Langley Park high on to the ridge above the valley where stands Quebec. The fanciful title bestowed on this hamlet by an Earl of Durham who sought to celebrate the victory of British arms seems a little odd now—and I daresay it must always have seemed so. Quebec, which sits squarely on Dere Street which is the ancient way from England to Scotland, once had a small pit employing a couple of hundred miners but all has been dead for years now. Behind the Hamsteels Inn the colliery rows, Chapel Street, Busty Street, and others have been bulldozed away and the people taken down into Langley Park. There really is no future for what remains of Quebec, as there cannot be for the nearby hamlet of Esh which also used to have its pit which is long gone. But Herbert says if he were rich (a bellowing ironic laugh here, since he does not believe in personal riches) he would build a house in Quebec looking down on Langley Park and his beloved Brownie Valley. "For one thing," he said, gazing at the isolation, and listening to the silence, "you'd never be overlooked, would you?"

5

Dead and Alive

FROM Langley Park it is a devious route to Quaking Houses. Indeed, it is devious and highly irregular to get to Quaking Houses from anywhere. It is, whichever way you approach it, a journey of ironic fantasy, and you cannot help but dwell in some wonderment on the place names of the unsalubrious villages you encounter. What self-confidence, *naïveté*, or marvellous insularity, for example, persuaded a community to name a place Bloemfontein? The village was arising, naturally, at the height of Boer War imperialism, and not only its name, but the name of each of its streets, Bloemfontein, Kimberley, Ladysmith, Standerton and Greylingstadt bear a somewhat grubby witness to this fact. But Bloemfontein, now as ever, bears no physical nor (I suspect) mental resemblance to anything South African. It is seemingly as ill-named as is Sunniside, another colliery village on another road not far away, through which Quaking Houses may also be approached. That is to say that the sky is mostly grey and the atmosphere, less lethal than when every pit in the area was active, but undeniably still a compound of grit, smoke and sulphur.

Bloemfontein, of course, as virtually all the villages in this bereft area of north-west Durham, is known in the planners' jargon as Category D, which means bluntly that it is destined to die. It is therefore an area of social blight which can only get worse, but despite all this there is an aura about the place, and whenever I pass that way I am struck with what an author of Dickensian imagination might concoct about it. Alternatively, a latter-day Arnold Bennett might find the area just as enriching or as creatively exciting as anything that emerged from the Five Towns. Certainly the ugliness is so positive as to be endearing; certainly, also, the dire lack of amenity and the seeming acceptance of this lack, brings a depression entirely lacking in pit areas of more optimistic mood.

The villages around the small town of Stanley, of which Quaking Houses is the more remote, have undergone in the last thirty
or forty years such profound changes as to render them almost
unique. For you had there perhaps twenty pits, each with its substantial complement of men at work, each with its miners' lodge,
each with its limited but vivid village life which depended utterly
on the pit. There was the Busty, the Edward, the Oswald and the
Thomas, the Billy Pit, the Hedley, the Louisa and the Drift Mine.
There was the Beamish Mary and the Morrison North and South,
and those at East Tanfield and Tanfield Colliery, not to mention the
small place at Burnhope. There were others, too, but they are all
gone now: there are no pits anywhere near. It was, in its time, a
remarkable area in which the same seam of coal moved from one
pit to the other, and in which the king was the hand hewer who
operated in the thin seam. Before the machinery came it was conceivably the hardest job in the world to labour in the Harvey
seam or the Brockwell, each of which was about twenty inches
high, and hundreds did so. In one way it was a simple life and in
another complex, for in each village each lodge negotiated its own
production price with management. They all differed; some lodge
officials striking good bargains, and other bad. But there was one
certain truism which was not negotiable and that was that you
had to labour long for a living wage. And this was true in Bloemfontein, in Quaking Houses, in South Moor and Craghead and
Beamish which also had a few streets nearby which were called
No Place. No Place? Again you imagine the pawky, self-deprecat-
ing pitmatic humour in evidence, for No Place, really, has never
had the smallest of pretensions.

They are all within a few miles, every place I have mentioned
so far, and they had masses in common in the halcyon days before
productivity and cost became so crucially significant and before the
thin seams ran out. Now they are like a band of hopeless brothers.

The pits have gone, the older miners have taken their early
retirements, and the younger men have gone on to other things.
Some new industry has been established and miners have quickly
learned to make batteries and ball bearings. In the clubs which
enjoy such big prosperity, the ex-miners in their eternal conversa-
tions with marras insist that they would not go back to the pits,
not even to the coal face where now they can make some real
money. This is overwhelmingly the favourite topic of conversation. But some, of course, have become the miner-commuters of
the '70s: you see them waiting for the NCB buses on dark

mornings to take them to Marley Hill and New Herrington, and even as far as the big pits on the coast.

But back to Quaking Houses, the archetypal pit village that is dying—how did it get its curious name? There are two theories. The first is that the original houses—Victorian cottages grouped around the pit head—were so jerry built that they literally quaked and fell down within an astonishing short time of being built. The second is that they fell because of the subsidence caused by colliery workings. Present-day inhabitants are both incurious and un-informative about this: suffice it that Quaking Houses has a name which conjures up a vision of a vanished day.

Quaking Houses has had a constant supply of sportsmen, foot-ballers especially, subscribing therefore to the saying that at one time if you needed a footballer of quality you merely shouted down the pit shaft—and a dozen came up. It once had the world-champion quoits player, Harry Rostron, who is still spoken of with pride, and its football team, ironically named the Quaking Houses Lillywhites, performed prodigies in local leagues. It had its period of being politically 'red', as had so many pit villages in Durham; it had two volunteers to the Spanish Civil War both of whom died. For one night Keir Hardie stayed in the village to discuss the shape of the new Socialist Utopia—but he was away bright and early in the morning.

At Quaking Houses if you take a step further the fells engulf you—and this has meant a good and honest poaching tradition—but even this has diminished to nothingness.

Nowadays the young people complain that there is nothing to do unless you drink hard or are an addict of bingo. Vandalism is pretty ferocious, too, since too many kids are bored and aim-less, and all efforts to get a community centre failed because this, of course, is Category D—and that makes them untouchable. Other negative facts that emerge include the closing of the Co-op, the Methodist Chapel and one of the two pubs.

The colliery reservoir was filled in after a drowning, the lodge banner is in the keeping of the miners' HQ at Durham, and the colliery band exists only by proxy as its musicians have been absorbed and re-absorbed elsewhere as every pit in sight seemed to have closed.

A sophisticate of my acquaintance who was born and brought up in Quaking Houses and now inhabits the world said, "If you're an outsider I dare say you're appalled. As for me, my mum still lives there, and therefore, lousy as it is, it's home."

D

From Quaking Houses to Easington is, I suppose, about twenty-five miles across the flat face of pitmatic Durham. The physical journey takes about forty-five minutes, but if you travel philosophically, economically, and giving due consideration to matters of the spirit, then one is light years removed from the other.

Quaking Houses is dead; Easington is tumultuously alive. One is absolutely of the past; the other, while acknowledging a past filled with the fabric of tragedy, looks squarely and (as far as I could judge) happily, at an exciting future. Comparisons are virtually endless. The old congregate in Quaking Houses; Easington, increasingly, is a place for the young. In Quaking Houses, when they talk of the pits, it is reminiscently, and all the memories of a past life are invoked. At Easington you tend to hear the terms of modern technology. Phrases like 'computer time' are not unheard of and references to 'high capacity shearers' and '£5m modernization schemes' occur logically enough in conversation about the pit. One must be careful, however, not to pursue these analogies too far, tempting though the prospect may be. For experiences may be as separate as the continents, but the people, really, are the same; that is to say they have the obsessive friendliness of the Durham miner, and a desire to communicate what they know, forthrightly but without pretension. I never heard one of them boast.

At Easington one dull May morning a quarter of a century ago the pit was torn apart by the greatest mining disaster in modern times. That, together with all the scrimping and starving and protesting, is their heritage and their past. Now at Easington they are a pregnant part of the remarkable revolution which is tackling all the vast coal reserves under the North Sea. That is the present and the future. Perhaps the greatest conditioner, the palpable, momentous fact which brings both optimism and (sometimes) arrogance in its wake, is that there are 550 million tons of coal to be extracted from under the North Sea at the very least.

Easington Colliery (and this also applies to all the other big Durham pits to the north and south of the village) will not close down until all that coal is out.

This knowledge is a heady medicine indeed; knowing that in two decades, or three or four, the pit will still be there, unless immense changes which cannot at present be foreseen take place. For a community dynamically concerned to preserve its identity, and conscious at the same time of all the disappearing mining entities in Durham, this spells security. It is probably the only time in their history that this feeling has been so widely apparent, and that is why Easington and its nearby neighbours of Horden and Blackhall and Dawdon and Seaham have a sense of their uniqueness.

Their grandfathers would never have recognized their enviable situation: good wages which will only get much higher—and not a redundant miner in sight. Indeed the reverse is now the case. The National Coal Board in Durham advertise widely for miners to return to the pits and for boys to take up the career. The pictures thus painted are perhaps a little more glowing than they deserve to be. But all this propaganda is with the likes of Easington in mind.

Still, as ever in a mining community, there is little outward evidence of these heartening facts. The place does not smell prosperous. The old miners sit on the seats amid the dust and petrol fumes of the main road, but oblivious to these trifling hazards. They exude toughness, are polite to intrusive strangers like myself and reminisce eternally, often enough about old times and about the classic and terrible disaster of May 1951. It was the last great tragedy of the Durham coalfield. Since then so massive have been the improvements both in ventilation and in roof supports that it is inconceivable—and almost impossible—that such a tragedy should occur again.

What happened was that just after dawn on 29th May in the Five Quarter Seam there was a sudden congregation of fire damp at the coal face. The massive explosion which resulted either killed or entombed (and therefore condemned to a lingering death) eighty-one men to which subsequently had to be added two rescue workers. It was the first disaster in Easington's history, and once it had happened there was brought into play all the classic ingredients of pit tragedy of which—thankfully—most people were only historically aware.

Men in other seams, unaffected, were brought from their work to the pit bottom and then into the light of day. The ambulances were marshalled; the rescue teams called to duty. Quickly the word blazed round the sleepy village. Rumour was rampant, and could not really be checked because, for long enough, nobody was really precisely aware of what had happened. Then when the extent of the tragedy became apparent there could only be hope that the rescue teams, who faced the hazard of pit gases, would break through the mountain of rock in time to ensure that some at least of the trapped men would still be alive.

Wives and families gathered silently at the pit top, just as they
have been depicted in countless scenes of earlier days when explosions as we have seen were lamentably frequent. I was there and
waited with the wives and their children and it was both remarkable and moving to see the stoicism and bravery of their demean-
our. It was at least twelve hours before the names of those miss-
ing could be released, and forty hours exactly before Mr Sam
Watson, then the General Secretary of the Durham Miners Union,
stood at the pit gates, removed his hat and said, "We must now
take it for granted that there is no hope for these men."

Nor was there, as everyone knew in their hearts there could
not be. But there was still the slow enactment of tragedy. For the
rescue workers did get through, of course. The bodies were recovered and brought to the surface, and buried together in that
Garden of Memory in the Easington Cemetery.

And then there was the magnificent public reaction: a positive
Niagara of pennies, shillings and pounds, so that within six
months there was £200,000 to provide for the eighty-two widows
and eighty-seven children. To this day there are widows receiving
a weekly allowance.

Then came the public enquiry during which, day after day, the
scene had to be redrawn and the story retold. Until, eventually,
it was all over, judgement was pronounced (highlighting faults
in organization at the colliery) the disaster faded even from the
inside pages, and Easington could resume the business of living
without the handicaps of massive publicity. People craved a
decent obscurity—and this they have had for twenty-five years.
Yet comparing the village outwardly with what it was on the day
of the disaster, nothing much seems to have changed. Past the
old men one swings down a long incline: "One mile to the
colliery," they say, but it is much further than that. Past the
supermarkets and the bingo halls and the clubs and a fair amount
of urban tattiness to what I like to think of as the colliery house
enclaves.

For there they all are; ranks of small homes cascading in their
narrow rows down towards the sea: The 'A's—Angus, Alma,
Argent Streets, then the 'B's—Biddy, Bolam and Bradley, then the
'C's—Court, Chandler and Cowell. Confusing you would think,
but they used to be known by numbers, and then a stranger, not
to mention some of the villagers, had real trouble trying to find
a friend. The colliery houses look the same but, as they say, they
are palaces inside nowadays. A few years ago the local branch of

the union did a deal with the NCB and as a result inside lavatories and a hot-water system was installed in every colliery house
in the village. For this each miner pays a sort of mortgage which
amounts to sixty pence a week for twenty years. But Bob Garside,
one of the union officials who negotiated the agreement, says
that there was objection from the diehards. "They said this was
the thin end of the wedge actually paying for home improvements.
If we didn't watch out we'd be getting rent books, and where
would the miner's traditional right to a rent free home be
then. . . ."

Now the pit houses have fitted carpets and colour TV, and most
of the requisites of comfort. They are as far removed from Railway
Street in Langley Park with its outside netties as can conceivably be imagined. If you want a guide to material progress then
here it is.

To live in the enclave at Easington means that, at most, you
are ten minutes quiet walk from the pit head—in Bob Garside's
case he could sprint it in a moment or two. But actually getting
to work is far more difficult than that. At Easington the seven
and a half hour shift is reduced by two hours each day because
it takes an hour to get to the pit face—and, of course, an hour
back. Once the miners get to the bottom of the pit shaft there is
about a five mile journey 'in bye' that is to the place where the
coal is extracted. Nowadays the miners travel by high speed train
which is not unlike an austere form of underground. This ride
takes about half an hour and then there is a walk to the pit face
which takes up to twenty minutes. Once this used to be accomplished by a crouch and a scramble because the roof was so low;
nowadays the miners walk upright and in dignity.

It is at the face that the differences in mining are at their most
dramatic and comparisons are most sensational. Peter Lee, one of
the most radical of the miners' leaders of the past in Durham
used to call eternally for a greater ease in a miner's life and for
"some expedient" that would alleviate the crushing labour. Now
if he came back and saw the five-feet seams at Easington and the
power-loading teams cutting coal in great swathes he would see a
prayer answered. But he would acknowledge as every foreigner
like myself must do that it is only easier by comparison with what
has gone before. For all car workers, street sweepers, company
executives, solicitors, journalists and book writers the message
is explicit: it remains no place for weaklings. Actually the miners,
working in teams of ten or twelve, adapt quite easily to the opera-

tion of these magnificent machines, high-capacity shearers as they are called, and worth about a quarter of a million pounds each. But why does the old miner turn so easily to the new technology? Well, it is partly a physical and partly a mental thing, and does not only operate when applied to pit matters. The miner is a marvellously quick learner when he quits the pit for any other job. Everything, you see, seems easier than when he nearly broke his back wielding a hand pick for a pittance. Thus he approaches his new job in the modern pit conscious of its many advantages. It is true that he still may be shattered by noise when operating the shearer and showered in the same old noxious dust. But who notices the noise if you have always had to have a special sign language because of the racket at the old pit face? Who bothers with the dust if it has been your constant companion? But if you have the pit in your bones, you are profoundly thankful that nowadays you do not have to wield a pick until your senses reel, or hack away with a shovel until every muscle rebels. These are the credits of the new mining age to which you must add the repository of pit sense possessed by every good miner. It is not easy to analyse but is really common sense as applied to pit matters.

He applies this nous to the new situation, boosted psychologically by the knowledge that he does not have to be the strong man in the circus any longer to come through a shift without a weariness which seems like the end of the world. Added to these fortunate circumstances is the happy knowledge that labour relations at colliery level (whatever confrontations may be going on in the country) are characterized by a democratic ease. There are no baby starvers, which was the old miner's term for the hard-faced official who would lay you off if you crossed him, and deputies and overmen, who have not always been the most popular of mortals, could not be petty dictators even if they tried. Nowadays, of course, they do not want to try.

All this is a measure of the change. It would be as utterly surprising to the old mining martyrs as if my grandfather (who would have been 120) were to come back, silver beard, patrician Edward VII profile and all, be given a ride in an Aston Martin and see a colour TV set showing a blast-off for the moon.

There is all this and the security I mentioned before which can be illustrated in a different way. For instance there are 90 million tons of coal recoverable by the Easington pit alone, so that, even if you reckon on production going sky-high in the years ahead, there will still be pit work in the village at the end of the first half of the twenty-first century. An exciting prospect if you consider that they are pushing the pit face out with those marvellous shearers five feet further under the North Sea every day. Who knows this way where they will all end up? So you can reason that even when the North Sea oil boom is over, and we have pumped the wells dry, there will still be coal to mine, and the miner will still be treated with respect and in some quarters with awe. This is the revolution.

The pit publicists of the National Coal Board describe this situation in the glowing and sometimes specious terms of the advertising copywriter, but you wonder about personal happiness. When the miners first received paid holidays in the late 1930s the whole of Easington removed themselves to seaside resorts like Redcar a few miles further south. The holiday was planned weeks before, endlessly discussed, deliriously anticipated by the children. There is nothing like this scarcely subdued excitement now. For a week, the miners and their families solemnly met their marras on the seafront or while having a paddle, and talked their pit talk in the Redcar hostelries instead of the club.

Now the exodus is incredibly diverse, usually by plane from Newcastle and Teesside airports. So much so, indeed, that some of the children at least are more expert on the geography of the Costa Brava than of their own corner of Durham County. But the excitement is gone.

Bob Garside remembers with nostalgic affection (and he is only in his early forties) the picnics on the sand dunes nearby, the long walks they took as teenagers, and the delightful habit of sitting in the back row at the pictures. Nowadays there are no picnics, and the children, in a curious way, are less adventurous, move less far afield, and seem to stick close to home, back street and telly. Nobody walks, and you cannot go to the pictures because all the three cinemas are closed.

The teenager miner, eighteen or nineteen, unquestionably drinks a lot more. In Garside's day you graduated gradually to acceptance at the club, and certainly in your teens, you went there only once a week. Nowadays they go every night. Twenty-five years ago the kids went to Sunday school, but unless they are Roman Catholic, precious few go to any sort of church now.

Now, of course, bingo is the great entertainer for the women, and there are rumblings by some of the older generation about latch-key kids as a result of this addiction.

Bob Garside remembers his own mum, who would not have known the name of bingo and who had six sons and three daughters. He describes her, rather like the evaluation of a production manager: "She was always on the floor. In my childhood she never seemed to go to bed. Sometimes very late at night I'd wake up and creep to the top of the stairs and look down and there was my mother crying. I used to wonder about this, and it wasn't until I was a teenager that I realized that she was crying because she sometimes didn't know how she was going to manage—even the next day."

Not long ago the old lady was invited by relatives to live a lotus-eating life in America. The relatives are virtual millionaires, and they treated her like a queen, moving her around romantic places in Texas and the far South-west. They wanted her to stay, but she would not.

"I couldn't live that kind of life," she said as she returned thankfully to Easington.

This is how it is. People want to come back, and even the youngest generation do not want to go away. So boys usually ignore opportunities that may glitter and beckon them to a wider world. There is, in fact, no sign of a break with tradition. At Easington, where the miners are now secure, their boys go down the pit. If it lies anywhere that is where happiness is to be found.

6

From Club to Seaside

A n old miner of my acquaintance, long dead now, had an eminently practical way of getting home from the club after imbibing
too well.

With closing time past, and after his regulation ten pints of
strong beer, he carefully negotiated the back entrance of the club
and walked tentatively across a narrow, quiet lane to the back gate
of his garden. From the gate to the door of his colliery cottage
there was a narrow brick path perhaps thirty yards long on either
side of which grew his leeks, his cabbages, his potatoes. There was
the additional hazard of his greenhouse with his prize tomatoes
growing marvellously inside. Walking up this path, ten pints of
beer inside you and the bricks uneven under foot, a pitch black-
ness ahead of you, it was fatally easy to stumble and end sprawled
on the black soil, breaking the cabbage stalks, and perhaps ruin-
ing the best leek of all, of such immense girth and firmness that
no other grower could have approached its size. You could even
falter before the greenhouse, afflicted suddenly with a lack of
balance, and crack one of the panes of glass with your flailing
arms; after all, it had happened before. So the old man, denying
indignantly that he was ever drunk and saying that it was only
old age that made his feet sometimes escape him, fixed a stout
cord to his garden gate and linked the cord tautly to a stake sunk
in the soil every few yards until the last piece of cord linked the
last stake with the door knocker of his house. So then, each Friday
and Saturday night, which were the only times when this aid was
remotely necessary, he grasped the cord at the garden gate and,
announcing his impending arrival with throat-clearing which
grew steadily louder, he was guided cautiously along the path to
the safety of his living-room and the sausages which sizzled for
his supper.

You could say he was beguiled by the club, that the talk in the quiet corner of the bar was so deeply interesting and the domino playing of such surpassing subtlety that time flashed away and he was overcome by his inebriations almost in spite of himself. You could say all this with truth because the club is virtually all things to all men in a pit village. It is also the subject, almost everywhere, of a remarkable revolution.

The old idea was of a drinking club for men only in which scant attention was paid to decoration or comfort. A chair (more probably a bench) to sit in solemn drinking rows; a table upon which to set the serried rank of pint glasses. That was it, although dominoes (as I have indicated) were frivolously permitted. The great occasions were the flower show, the leek show, the racing of the whippets and the pigeons. The old miner attending such a club never took his wife out anyway—and even if he had she (usually being a miner's daughter herself) would never have dreamed of going to the club.

Then came the revolution, or more particularly the radical changes in the Licensing Acts of 1961. These resulted in clubs being advised not only to admit women but actively to encourage their membership. From that moment the old-style drinking club was doomed, and the integration of the club fully within the community began to happen.

"It was ten years before I could persuade my wife to go to the club; now I can't keep her away," a miner at Quaking Houses exclaimed in mock exasperation. He might have added that now she is chairman of the ladies' committee, and that schemes of decoration, choice of curtain material and carpets are delegated to her.

Carpets, it need only be added, were unheard of in the old colliery drinking clubs. As for curtains—well, it was reluctantly acknowledged that you needed something, preferably the cheapest of materials to cover the windows. Refinements like this tended to be of a makeshift nature, since their lack was likely to be unnoticed.

But slightly more than a decade in which there has been unrestricted access for women, and several years at least when they have been actively welcomed, has transformed attitudes and wrought changes which are seen by some to be miraculous. The drinking den full of male chauvinistic spirits has become the social centre around which almost all the leisure activities of the colliery village revolves. Close down the club and there is nothing.

Sociologists from the South visit the clubs because, of course, there is nothing remotely like them in Esher or Pinner or Penzance. Earnest researchers from universities in the United States spend vacations looking into the 'phenomenon' of the club. What fascinates them and makes them envious is the way in which working-class people create what are, in effect, substantial businesses, the control of which is exercised entirely by voluntary labour. Committees (some are called boards of directors) consider the implications of turnovers which can be as much as £300,000 a year. I spent an evening with just such a board, pitmen to a man. All the time the secretary was making decisions of the calibre and significance of an executive in middle management. In his working life he is at the coal face. The clubs blossom in an incredible way. Almost without exception the 346 clubs in Durham County whether huge (with membership up to 5,000) or less than one tenth of that size, are confronted with the problems and pleasures of prosperity.

They are all members of a business amalgam known as the Club Union. They are also shareholders in a brewery (the Federation) which brews largely for them and therefore enables them to sell the beer and most other liquors at prices below those in the competing public houses. The Fed., as it is universally known, also pays a dividend on sales which amounts to £4.50 on each barrel of beer. Each barrel contains 288 pints, and if your requirement is a humble half pint occasionally, then you may wonder if consumption can ever be big enough to make the 'divi' worth while. I was asked this same question in 'The Bull and Bush' in Hampstead where a polyglot group of young men nursed half pint glasses for an age. Actually it is not uncommon for a large club to dispose of twenty barrels a week which is more than 5,000 pints, bringing a rebate of more than £100.

The clubs are non-profit making by law, but they cannot avoid amassing huge surpluses. They are eternally moving house from premises they have outgrown to new buildings which, often enough, are of a surpassing luxury. Capital borrowed from the Fed. at advantageous interest terms finances these projects. When they are paid off and the deeds handed over, it is the occasion for a celebration, Deed parties can last for three successive nights when beer is free, as are the sandwiches and chicken legs, and everyone is filled with the euphoria of achievement.

New buildings cost up to £200,000; renovation schemes (the addition of a ballroom or a balcony for example) cost up to

£70,000. Enterprises of this sort now occur so frequently as to make scarcely any news outside the colliery village where the new building is arising. Inside the new club there will be several bars each tastefully and expensively furnished. The ballroom will have its stage and its theatrical ceiling and the acoustics will be superb. In the ballroom when there is no dancing there will sometimes be a cinema. The clubs have taken on this facility as the cinemas have closed outside. Films are modern—(the latest James Bond but one, for example) and the cost of admission is about half what it would be in a commercial cinema.

There is a variety show, or, as they say in the colliery vernacular in Durham, 'torns' a couple of times each week. This especially applies to a Sunday evening which is the peak entertainment night. Although proceedings do not open until 7 p.m. when they are permitted by the licensing laws to begin selling beer, the queues begin to form at 5.30 p.m. for admittance an hour later. The evening will begin with half an hour of bingo which will have big prizes. Then comes the real entertainment which attains the highest professional standards.

More and more the star system is being adopted, and nationally known entertainers, coming to the new commercial night clubs in the county, do a round of the colliery clubs as well. They can get £80 a night; even the top local entertainers expect £50. Such a man is Bobby Thompson, a diminutive comedian who has had several attempts to reach national eminence but has now happily settled for the highly lucrative local round. He is known as the 'little waster', and has a Durham pitmatic accent, and an irreverent, family type of approach which is very popular. There are pop groups by the score many of them straining ambitiously for national recognition and all of whom seem to have agents. Negotiations with all these people, the planning of the proper mix of entertainment and the scheduling weeks and months ahead, is another of the complex duties fulfilled by one or other of the honorary directors.

Elsewhere in the club, away from intrusive music and singing, the conversationalists, the pool players, and the coloured TV addicts meet. So do the members of the various societies. The leek growers may be discussing the latest monster stand of leeks of perhaps 160 cubic inches which has led to the award of Champion of Champions at the show. The darts players may pore over the league tables, the whist, cribbage, and even bridge players quietly contain themselves in little coteries. Here and there a chap sits with his cap on. The footballers come in from training, and talk obsessively about football. They take it very seriously and if this is the night before the Saturday match there will be no drinking. The cricketers, in season, are hugely content with their towering position in the league, and the cup reposing on the sideboard indicating that they are village champions of Britain; the pigeon and whippet men gossip in their abstruse verbal shorthand, and the club secretary for the tenth time that night listens courteously to a request or a complaint and makes a decision. A few clubs are evolving away from all this, and founding restaurants instead; places which serve steak and scampi and have piano players tinkling the cabaret tunes of the '30s. But most are content with so filling the social void in the village in the manner described that people, truly, would be lost without them.

Old Harry, which was the name of the miner who fixed up the cord to help him on his way, used to sit with his cap on in his club—and he never looked remotely out of place. I cannot conceive though, what he would make of the club I am in as I write these words which, in addition to most of the felicities I have mentioned, has a gracious Georgian-type façade which sometimes they light up at night. To Harry, after ten pints of strong beer, I dare say they would have looked like the lights of heaven.

To contemplate writing about the seaside villages of Durham is to be forced, almost in spite of oneself, into a compendium of errors. One has to look closely at the use of words and to consider like Joad what we mean by both a 'village' and 'the seaside'.

Recently the organizers of a village cricket competition promoted nationally by a firm of whisky distillers queried whether a place known as Bomersund (which happens to be in Northumberland) could be known as the village it was claiming to be. They did this because Bomersund, winners of the competition against much fancied opposition from the South the previous year, looked like winning again. Some places of fairer aspect and incontestably more villagey pretensions were naturally questioning their right to do so. Additionally there was a puzzlement as to whether a place which is indistinguishable from all around it in a mass of urban housing had not forfeited its right to be called a village if, indeed, such a right or privilege had ever been bestowed upon it. I must confess that having driven through the place, sipped the ale and watched the arrogant cricketers at play, the same thought had crossed my mind.

What happened in the case of Bomersund is irrelevant but its categorization (it is still known, apparently, as a former colliery village) is useful since there are many places in Durham which are indubitably by the sea but which (by the most romantic stretch of imagination) would not be described as watering places, resorts, or (unless the case of Bomersund is duly heeded) villages.

What is undoubted is that Durham possesses wide stretches of sandy beaches untainted (except on rare occasion) by any sort of pollution, safe for bathing and patronized by the multitude. There is not the vestige of a beach like Brighton or Margate from South Shields to Seaton Carew. When the Dunelmian leans over the pier at Brighton or Lyme Regis and contemplates the shingle beneath, he is confounded, often enough, as to how the populace can be enjoying their stay by the sea "with all those stones".

The people of Durham, thus, will go to the seaside within their county boundary conscious of some superiority, the golden sand being indeed almost universal. In other respects, and from a pro-fusion of parochial pride, they may also be prepared to defend their coastal limitations. Thus the east wind which prevails all summer long may make the temperature plunge from a benign seventy degrees fahrenheit a mile or two inland to a cooling fifty-five. This, despite the goose pimples it causes as you sit in your bikini or your shorts, is described as 'healthful' and 'bracing'—adjectives which people from more accommodating climates may care to dispute.

These fundamentals apart, and despite the increasing sophistica-tion caused by the package tour to Spain and Majorca, the traveller to the seaside in Durham still has a sense of occasion, a feeling of excitement, and in a true sense the thought that he is escaping from industrial blight and tedium to more open and carefree places. Even—and it is my purpose so to argue—a sense of going to the village which happens to be by the seaside.

But how is this? You may look down the map from the mouth of the Tyne to the great maw of the Tees, and of all the names, some of which are both evocative and pretty, none describes a watering place of charm and distinction, or a resort anyone has ever heard of. Aside from Whitburn, more famous, and described thus in another chapter as a place of rural charm, there is not a village—at any rate in the acceptable sense—in sight. Unless, that is, Easington is a village (which it is, because the big colliery is there and we have already written about it). There is also Horden or Seaham or Blackhall where roughly the same yardstick applies, and Crimdon which is all caravans and must be something.

There is no genteel history of the watering place such as may be found only a little further south at Whitby or Scarborough; no crude Regency cartoon showing the licentious common people spying on the gentlemen cavorting in the surf in the nude; no occasion for the rhymster to observe sadly, as he did of the bathing belles of Scarborough, around 1745:

"The ladies dressed in flannel cases,
Show nothing but their handsome faces."

No incidence in Durham of the dippers, those necessary people in more presumptuous seaside places who dragged you from your bathing machine and dumped you, for your own good under the waves and nothing to tell us of the evils of mixed bathing at Roker or Crimdon (we get the story *ad nauseam* from everywhere else) with the implication that the gentlemen, thus separated, could be placed nearer to the spot where the main drainage pipeline poured its contents under the waves. Durham is bereft of fashionable seaside history. You may look in vain—in Wheelan's *History of the County Palatine of Durham* published in the 1890s, for example (it is exhaustive on any other topic) for references to seaside Durham. Roker, it is true, is a "pleasant marine suburb with a promenade and causeway just complete." But Seaburn, which nowadays has a dolphinarium and golf centre and promenade kiosks in serried ranks like Daleks, rates no mention at all. And Hendon, so beloved of our great, great-grandfathers: what has happened to Hendon? The truth is, of course, that none of them were 'seaside'. They were just by the sea and people went there without fuss and without fashion. You could walk from the mill at Fulwell village a mile from the sea down a rural road to the flat beach where the burn trickled into the sea. Thus Seaburn before the dolphinarium, and Roker, where the cliff grew higher, where the first of a succession of ravines petered out at the sea, and where there was only village and church until the shipowner and shipbuilders erected their villas, and where a few boarding houses grew and, for a few brief years, it became fashionable to stay.

This is the beginning of Durham's coastal strip which Surtees describes as bare and dreary. So it may be. It is not my purpose to invest it with any false glamour. But there have been times of both attainment and of ambition. Roker and Seaburn adorned their high old days with miniature illuminations, guidebooks written in English (and with a foreword inconsequentially in Esperanto) and amenities which in inflationary times read like offerings from some other Eden. Hire of swimming costumes (this was in 1939) one penny a time: deck chairs threepence a day, and you could get a return rail ticket from Burnley for £1 0s. 7d.

But what, I have asked, of Hendon? This is on the other side of the Wear and has been perplexed for years by a rampant erosion. Thus its cliff face increasingly has been falling into the sea and the puny beach is studded with rocks and segments of clay. Now they have built a sea wall as protection against further depredation, and when you wander over the old railway line and see the excavations, the houses that are tumbling down, and hear of the high concentration of villains the area possesses, you may be excused—if a brisk north-easter is blowing—for deriding romantic suggestions that this ever has been a village. Yet, only faintly perceptible, the signs remain of the village of scattered farms and gardens it used to be. I stood on an evening of billowing sea fret on the Hendon Moor which was a verdant stretch when Victoria came to the throne, but is sadly battered now and soiled by industrial dross. Early Methodist evangelists used to preach there; they were prosecuted by irreligious authorities for "damaging the herbage". By the side of the verdure was the pleasant cliff top walk, and looking out to sea:

> "Fower colliers lay in Hendon Bay,
> At anchor for the tide.
> The Saucy Jane, the Eden Main,
> The Fox and the Rover's Bride"

A pleasant country path led to the beach from the Hendon Road then named Cutty Throat Lonnen. Hendon village, though, and we are talking now of the very beginning of the nineteenth century, was even then in danger though absolutely nobody realized it. Indeed optimism reigned. Superior people began to come for the bathing and there was also a tiny spa. People who drank these waters (and the mind reels at the vision) stayed at the Bath Hotel—and for a few years the village scene was set, seemingly immutable.

It was all so terribly misleading, of course. The exclusivity of Hendon village was shattered by the Industrial Revolution. The maze of country roads that separated Hendon from the main town of Sunderland was gobbled up. In fifty years—to 1850—the population of Hendon multiplied tenfold whereas that of Sunderland increased by only one hundred and fifty per cent. The tiny spa was swallowed by the building of the docks. The mansions became Victorian tenements and one of them was a reformatory for errant girls. By 1861, at the time of a census, 11,000 people lived in Hendon and the village was lost forever. But village it undoubtedly used to be.

At Ryhope, a mile or two south, the evidence of the village that was is more obvious. There is the fragment of a green, though since this is on the fringe of the A19 to Teesside, one is in danger of asphyxiation by petrol fumes if one lingers there. Ryhope is another former colliery village, the pit having long gone—but what about its claims to seaside eminence? William Fordyce, writing in the 1850s says it has "several good houses, well adapted for visitors during the bathing season", and adds that Ryhope Bay "affords good shelter for bathing machines." Thereafter news of the evolution of the village is scanty; indeed I have found none. Now, though, there is a surprising reward for the persistent enquirer. One needs to forge away from the A19 on to the direct coastal road to Seaham. Do this and the traffic dies away immediately, and though there is a curious salty awareness, there is still no immediate sign of the sea. This facility the villagers are obviously intent on keeping to themselves for you have to turn under a bridge (it is peppered with urban graffiti) upon which the coastal railway runs. This was a fortuitous manoeuvre, since there are no direction signs. Once past the bridge though, a different world emerges. A gentle ravine, the banks of which are alive with wild flowers and colourful weed, and a stream running at the foot. Cows in green fields above, and mushroom gatherers profitably engaged. A few yards of winding pathway and there, indeed, is the beach, with children energetically defying the goose pimples. A poor thing this beach, really, though better beaches, steeper and more beautiful ravines, and romantic evidence of the past is certainly in prospect only a little further south.

Seaham is a couple of miles away, and this should not be confused with Seaham Harbour next to it which was entirely a nineteenth-century creation of the Londonderrys—a community contrived so that coal could be expedited to London and Europe.

Before Seaham there is a grander ravine which you enter by thirty-nine steps handily placed there by the council. Penetrate this ravine, walk the flowering, almost haunted path to the beach

E

200 yards away where the sand is smooth and yellow, and the light suddenly blinks upon you, and you reflect that this is a fairyland for imaginative schoolboys. But perhaps they are blasé, or there are too many ravines (they being characteristic of this coast) for this is the height of the summer holiday season and there are no boys.

There is another ravine at Seaham, and wide green cliffs and several hundred yards of golden yellow sand. There is also, of course, the continuing evidence that Lord Byron walked here. I suppose the story is well enough known but it deserves a précis here. Lord Byron became stricken by the beauty of Anne Isabella Milbanke, a daughter of a local industrialist, and duly married her by special licence in the drawing-room of Seaham Hall on 2nd January 1815. It seems that before the troth was ever plighted, but as the hour approached, Byron either by doubt, or conscious of the momentous step he was taking, gave increasing range to his poetic temperament.

Consequently he moved restlessly far and wide through the grounds of Seaham Hall and even, it is said, penetrating to the beach, neurotically pondering his fate. In due course he returned for the ceremony in a daze, and emerged "as if from a sleep" when everything was concluded.

He was presumably still somewhat disorientated as they departed for the honeymoon for he enquired plaintively, "Miss Milbanke, are you ready?" This solecism was taken to be an ill omen. Thus it proved to be for Byron quickly tired to his bride and was soon apart from her, satirizing her cruelly in Don Juan as Lady Millpond.

Nowadays Seaham Hall is a hospital and the long road to New Seaham along its wall is known as Lord Byron's Walk. Hereabouts it is all clear, pristine, new, and even against a backcloth of Seaham Colliery, so close that the effect is almost claustrophobic, you can gaze at the sea, pick the wild flowers which stud the gently sloping green cliffs, and ponder the reason for the empty beaches even in the height of summer. The answer seems to be that people are spoiled by profusion. What would they do at Littlehampton or Southend or even Torquay with the unknown beaches of Seaham—as hard and firm as the gorgeous stretches of South Wales. They have tried for years to bring tourists in greater numbers to Northumbria—a publicity euphemism to describe Northumberland and Durham—and the lure they cast out, too heavily emphasized in my view, is of the castles and hills and the moors and the wildness usually in the far north. But the beaches from the borders of Scotland to those of Yorkshire are something near enough unique and still—despite all tourist efforts—virtually unknown, Of course there is a lack of amenity: a shortage of boarding house and of bingo, and of shows at the end of the piers, and there is that east wind. During my successive explorations, however, I had the rare good fortune to encounter a number of days when the wind, such as it was, coursed gently from the land. Then the beach was a balm, and at Crimdon, the extraordinary caravan village we shall presently explore, the benign conditions lent a raffish, indeed almost Hogarthian air to the proceedings. But first I continued away from the sea to another village of surprising aspect. For the major surprise, though, Dalton le Dale is best approached from the A19. Like Ryhope the turn-off brings immediate transformation from the urban blight and near dereliction of the highway to rural calm. There is yet another ravine here, miniature by comparison with most of the others, but fronting old houses with a rivulet at its base and tree-lined walkway. There is not much else to Dalton le Dale, which peters out soon enough at New Seaham, but there is a remarkable tribute paid to it by Ivan Way, a crippled miner who lived there all his life, and whose book charts the unremarkable but affectionate course life in the village had taken.

At Hesledon which one reaches soon enough, the social revolution can be seen in microcosm. The disused winding engine at the silent pit is the first reminder that the main purpose of this hamlet—to house the pitmen who walked to their work—is nowadays done. Further melancholia can be induced by the overgrown open spaces caused by the pulling down of old pit cottages, but there is a village green and upon it bright new houses. Thus the hamlet remains but it is a place that has lost its reason. The laudable attempt at reviving it somehow succeeds in making it more out of place than ever. One wonders what the future holds for former pit hamlets such as this of which there are dozens in Durham. Do you make them spruce and new again—or do you let them die? Probably you hope for the rampaging success of the new towns, and the gradual attraction of the young people to the fine new houses it is not too difficult to obtain within their boundaries. This way the old and ugly hamlets will die, and some already have. But talking to the old miners at Hesledon you sense that the struggle against this solution is less virulent than it used to be and that their ultra conservatism is being breached by events. There is no rhyme or reason about a place like Hesledon

except that it is the home of people who love it—unprepossessing though it seems to the outsider. The sense forcibly expressed
wherever I went was that this love grows less: another generation and it may have ceased altogether and Hesledon—and the
others—may be permitted to die.

There is not a vestige of sadness, however, in a fleeting visit to
Hawthorn, another hamlet of pleasance and calm a few hundred
yards off the noxious main road. Just a house or two, a farm and a
pub and then the road suddenly ends and the pathway to the sea
takes over. There is this way or yet another ravine and both
approaches to the shore end with a view of wildness and cliffs
deeply broken by the sea. Just offshore there are dangerous rocks
and shoals, and there is the bay, Hawthorn Hive, placid, as Hutchinson observed in the eighteenth century on a summer evening of
calm "when the moon is reflected on the smooth bosom of the
ocean."

But there was (and is) very much another side to this strange
ambiguous place. Hutchinson continues: "But when the storm lifts
the distracted waves, with a horrid gloom confounds the elements,
and mixes the spray even with the clouds; when the winds groan
in the caverns, and the hoarse billows thunder along the beach,
when the shrill cries of distress and wreck strike the ear from the
wretches without succour; when the affrighted cattle bellowing
leave the hills, and driving showers sweep the disconsolate landscape, little remains to make such a situation eligible." Fascination with the purple prose of Hutchinson need not mislead one
into doubting its approximate accuracy. This was a place of multitudinous wrecks, more than anywhere on the Durham coast. There
is the remarkable true story of the wreck of fifty small vessels on
5th November 1824, a day of fabulous storm. All crews perished
except that of the *Dido* which foundered between two rocks thirty
yards offshore. Major Anderson, a local gentleman and landowner,
mustered all his servants on shore, watching helplessly as the sea-
men in their broken boats tried unavailingly to throw ropes to
the shore. The major's Newfoundland dog, however, swam out in
the tumult, grabbed the rope from the *Dido*, and brought it back
to shore.

The fourteen members of the *Dido*'s crew thus were able to
come to safety. Next day the wife of the captain visited Hawthorn Hives cottage, the home of Major Anderson, to express her
gratitude and, in doing so, knelt down and kissed the dog.

The next surprise occasioned by popping off the A19 comes at

Castle Eden, though all but the most complete stranger who has completely neglected his homework must be prepared for the greatest ravine of them all. For all the great historians of the county are in awe of it and, in its modern setting, it has been seized and projected in the hectic name of tourism so that even, it is fondly anticipated, Europeans and peripatetic Americans may beat a path to its many entrances.

Certainly the situation is highly unusual with the ravine, filled with the sights, sounds and activities of nature, beginning at Castle Eden village and wending a mazy pathway for three miles and more to the sea. Now, as we shall see, this is a nature reserve of some consideration, and it is highly questionable as to whether it is appreciated as it ought. A couple of hundred years ago and less, though, it was simply a ravine which tested the extravagant prose of all the recorders of the time. Hutchinson, for example, excels even his description of Hawthorn, and Fordyce, not usually given to extravagance, writes of its wild natural beauty making it one of the romantic spots in the North. Certainly this is the longest dene and the cascade of water over the curious arrangement of rocks known as a Devil's Apronful is an oddity seen nowhere else in the coastal strip. But the sober Fordyce exaggerates, surely, in writing of "caves gloomy and unfathomable, and trees of every species that place themselves in the soil of Great Britain." In his day "gipsy parties are spread among the steep and grassy slopes seeking for a spot to display their picnic baskets. They gaze upward at the azure skies which they can only behold through the various clumps of trees that hang over them, forming a refreshing canopy to their repast." Other parties sought echoes with their wild halloos, and it is all staider and less remarkable now. But the Castle Eden Dene (why Eden and Dene since they mean the same?) is unknown in the wider context of the North, never mind the country, or Europe. No one is to blame for this, only the situation in the far forgotten North. How different if this were in Hampshire.

The Dene has been a local nature reserve for more than twenty years and is under the management of the nearby Peterlee New Town. They make the best of things, I suppose. I must say, though, that the North does not help itself too much. At either end of the Dene signposts are completely lacking. You may pass a dozen times—and I have done so—without being aware that the Eden Dene exists. However, they do dispense information: there are seventy species of birds, unique ferns, rare insects, mammals in reasonable profusion, and a castle of sorts which the public are not encouraged to visit. Pushing well into the castle grounds, however, I encountered a notice of deterrence I had not seen before. "Dogs loose" it said. I did not pursue the matter further. This, though, was at the farthest, landlocked end of the Dene, and I had forgotten, momentarily, that this was a chapter about the Durham seaside, and that there was, after all, a seaward end to the Dene about which almost all the historians had enthused. So I turned about, walked the full length of the Dene in heat and overpowering humidity, and in due course came to Denemouth or Deneholme, and straightaway to a grave disappointment.

Perhaps I expected too much, but all the other smaller ravines I had so far encountered on this expedition had ended with a sandy beach, usually deserted, and with an air, almost of conspiracy or guilt at having been discovered. There were golden sands a little to the north at Seaham; beaches, as we shall see (and which I already knew) at Crimdon and Carew. One anticipated, therefore, a gradual thinning of the close vegetation here on to a delectable and deserted Shangri La.

But there was not one. The Dene degenerated into scrubland, and where the beach should have been there is an unpleasant area of grey stony flatland upon which, on my visit, various natives sat despondently.

The beach used to be there, of course. Trips came; ice cream was sold; there were a few houses and a scouts' hut and there are plenty who will reminisce of the good old days when the beach was "as good as Crimdon". But over the years the waste from the huge collieries at Horden and Blackhall, dumped at sea, has been washed back here and now it is an area a bit like the surface of the moon.

The village of Castle Eden, I almost forgot to mention, has some nice old houses, a pub and a brewery, the engineering factory and colliery having long gone. There used also to be a limekiln in the Dene, and the felling of timber was a considerable local industry—so much so, indeed, that a ship, called the *Castle Eden* was built at Hartlepool with wood from the Dene.

There is little point, of course, in consulting oracles like Fordyce and Hutchinson about the next port of call since Crimdon, the caravan village, is very much the modern phenomenon. To reach it I passed quickly through Blackhall Colliery without comment since it is a colliery village or town as is Horden. Both boom with prosperity. The modes and manners, deficiencies and virtues of Easington are here repeated, and so is the dereliction, the immense influences of the club, and the parochial disregard of the outside world. A couple of miles south, though, the entrance to Crimdon introduces one to quite another world.

Crimdon squats—there is really no other word—along several hundred yards of the best cliffs in Durham. To the left are the rocks of Blackhall which can be observed more easily from the mouth of Castle Eden. These rocks assume some grotesque shapes with hollowed caves and cathedral-like structures. From there, past Crimdon and all the way to Hartlepool the beach is flat and smooth, soiled only by a fine peppering of coal dust. Above on the cliff top in high summer (when it was my good fortune last to pay a visit) Crimdon intently pursues its busy and vivid life. It is a tumultuous, bee-hive of a place and, at first glance, nearly as overcrowded—at any rate to the lover of solitude. There is perhaps, a gap of five yards between caravans along a frontage of several hundred yards, and the rows are repeated to the rear to the depth almost to the roadway. Some caravans are grand and described as élite seaside villas; others are unassuming and have names like Sea View I and Sea View II. Most are for hire and the population in peak months not only seethes, but changes with a weekend regularity. It was this maelstrom of people that I unwittingly chanced upon. There are amiable dogs by the score and of every parentage, all eager to insinuate themselves into raucous games. There are children by the thousand it seems, mostly aimless, lounging, lying, scrambling, spending extravagantly at the sweet shop.

They have nothing to do and quite happily are doing it. The beach, relatively speaking, is empty. The caravans, mostly, are full, and this is on a sunny midday. People sit and eat and watch TV; transistors blare; clothes are washed; babies fed; potatoes peeled, beer drunk out of the tops of bottles, and all within the compulsive, all-embracing view of everyone else. Old men in flat caps sit silently on benches facing the sea. Some families let the limited surroundings of their caravans become cluttered with the impedimenta of their lives. Others sweep and dust and even mow the grass of the cliff top and have little bowls with flowering geraniums. The scene, let me say it, is modern and urban but somehow Hogarthian, as I have indicated, in its gregarious abandon. People mingle—how they become enmeshed in each others lives! I watched two families arriving at adjoining caravans, each, until the moment of arrival, utterly unknown to each other.

There were four adults and half a dozen children, a sealyham terrier and an alsatian plus one blue budgerigar. Within minutes —and I swear it—the families became one mingling, joyous, noisy mass. The children were arranging games; the women talked animatedly over the non-existent garden fence, the topic as I shamelessly listened being previous holidays at Crimdon. Expertly they found out about each other, implied a mutual acceptance as neighbours, a joint condemnation at the ill behaviour of 'some' children, and the hope that it would continue fine. The men meanwhile had already arranged an expedition to the club, traded cigarettes and seen that they both carried the morning newspaper in which women's breasts are laid bare. These fundamentals acknowledged, an inspection of each other's identical caravans was solemnly carried out. First names were being used with utter naturalness, and only the alsatian and the sealyham retained a mutual and growling suspicion. The budgerigar, stricken by all this tumult, was both stunned and silent. This is the pattern, extreme in this instance, but observable everywhere. Crimdon is not for the standoffish, the socially aloof or those temperament-ally inclined to go on their own.

When the rains pour down, as it has been known to do, or the wind belts from the sea as it does much of the time, I imagine it must be very dreary indeed, though camp officials insist that their 'guests' make the best of it and emerge from any holocaust smil-ing and indomitable. If you ask people why they come to the caravan village of Crimdon year after year they tell you it is a change. It is certainly that.

So the journey down the coastal strip was almost over. There merely remained Seaton Carew which was just beyond the towering cranes of Hartlepool; ten minutes in fact from the cosiness of Crimdon. Seaton Carew, though, is very different, and if any-where on the Durham coast ever had pretensions to being a resort then this must have been it. The village, as all the historians will tell you, was a fashionable place for bathing from the middle of the eighteenth century, and had all the adjuncts required: genteel lodgings, bathing machines, the appropriate shops and the essential requirements of sophisticated leisure. It also had in the Seaton Hotel a place where the élite could assemble. There were balls at the Seaton to which it was by no means easy for ordinary people to receive invitations. I dare say that at one time Seaton Carew might have had an ambition to be a Scarborough, and it still, in truth, retains an air of faded charm to which the large grey houses which face the wide and gorgeously flat beach largely contribute. But of course it is a village no more, being sandwiched between the industry of Hartlepool and the Teesside colossus. A fragment of the village green remains, but several of the grey houses are old people's homes. Here the cliffs that have been our constant companion since Hendon have entirely receded, and Seaton Carew, when the air is warm and the bathing safe (which it almost always is) is in contrast to Crimdon, full of children enjoying the beach and bounding with delight.

7

South from the Tyne

THERE is a territory just south of the Tyne Bridge and therefore as far north in the county of Durham as you can get, which has long exerted a fascination upon me. There is perhaps one hundred square miles stretching as far east as White Mere Pool, veering south-west from Gateshead, then due south, then eastward to Pelton and Birtley. It is an area unpromising scenically speaking, but full of both character and surprise.

I spent a week looking for the secret places, identifying the villages that have vanished, those that have been submerged in the massive southward thrust of urban man, and assembling the fragmentary evidence of eighteenth- and nineteenth-century isolation that still survives. I captured a castle; scrutinized a remarkable gravestone and kept an encyclopaedia published more than a century ago always at my side. Then, every village I visited was throbbing with a vivid, dramatic, and sometimes rather obscene form of life. But what had happened to them today? Where, indeed, do we start, for there is a profusion of places hugging the fellside above the valley of the Team, or stretching away at slightly less an elevation from Lamesley to the land where the night silence used to be shattered by the sounds of the military tattoo?

In the floor of the valley where Gateshead ended there were green fields, the suggestion of a stony road, linking with the turnpike further on and the hamlet of Team where, so I believe, there was little except a public house and a couple of Methodist chapels. Here the transformation is most dramatic; the Team Valley Trading Estate no less; straight concrete roads for two miles; fifty factories. This is the basic, shattering change to Team country, for wherever you go, high on the fell or deep into the mysteries of Ravensworth, the hectic scene of the valley floor and the roads leading to it are laid open to you from every point of vantage.

Still, there is more than a suggestion of times past about Lamesley where the church (eighteenth century) hugs the roadside and where, indubitably, there used to be a village in what Fordyce calls "the pleasant vale of Team". There was a railway station, a pub, a school, a vicarage, a blacksmith's shop. Now the station is a marshalling yard, but mention of the vicarage leads one inevitably to that gravestone recording the death at the age of 100 in 1951 of the Rev. John Croft, Vicar of Lamesley from 1898 until he died, and by any standard a unique individual.

John Croft preached a rousing sermon the week before his end. When he was ninety-eight he was high on some ladders pruning fruit trees when the ladder snapped. However, he recovered from his fall and gave thanks for his recovery by what he described as a fitting form of indulgence: he read the New Testament through— in Greek. His wife, scarcely less remarkable, died shortly after him aged ninety-eight. They had been married seventy-five years.

All this land is part of the Ravensworth estate; the name indeed was stitched long ago into the fabric of northern life. For myself I remember an elder sister journeying to Ravensworth Castle to see the military tattoo. It was, for a year or two in the thirties, a compulsive part of the summer scene. Around here the Ravensworth influence is still evident to all. The Ravensworth Arms is a fine and worthy pub, though there are those who still sigh for the old hostelry it used to be. There is Ravensworth Grange and a house or two on a remote crossroad which (according to the ordnance map but there is no other visible indication) is Old Ravensworth. But there is no sign on any modern map I have ever seen of what little remains of Ravensworth Castle, which is curious because remains undoubtedly exist. But as you pursue your peregrinations in all directions with The Ravensworth Arms, roughly, at the centre, there is not the slightest sign anywhere of where the castle might have been. Simply you have to ask questions, get some mighty peculiar (not to say vacant) answers, and overcome some considerable deterrence before you can stand among the towering undergrowth and the tumbling stonework where, in the spacious days past, all was magnificence.

This I set out to do spurred on by a formidable curiosity, for I knew of the existence of a castle here, possibly since the thirteenth century, that it was rebuilt in light Gothic splendour in the first decade of the nineteenth century, and that subsequently, under the suzerainty of the second Baron Ravensworth, the most distinguished people in the land were entertained. The famous

Duke of Wellington slept here; so did Gladstone and Disraeli and Sir Walter Scott.

Why then should we not as we traversed Ravensworth territory be made easily aware that such a place existed? The Liddell family before they became ennobled as Ravensworths, were merchants, coalowners, Parliamentarians, and had a fair proportion of eccentrics in their ranks. For a wager Sir Henry-George Liddell, accompanied by a Mr Consett and a Mr Bowes travelled to Lapland in 1786, returning the same year accompanied not only by a herd of reindeer (which subsequently bred and thrived on the estate) but also by Sigree and Anae, two Lapland girls. It seems that without fuss or bother these children had left their families on the promise of being returned by the great English gentlemen. In England they happily survived the great curiosity of people of the Team Valley who came to marvel at their squat figures and broad features, and were, in due course, sent back home.

Ravensworth Castle, throughout the nineteenth century, seems to have been a social pinnacle towards which all the pushing early industrialists aspired. The carriages drove through the gates at Lady Park Lodge across the rolling parklands to the cultured grounds and lake surrounding the castle itself.

It was the rumbling underground that finally caused the castle almost to tumble down. The coal workings caused subsidence in the grounds; cracks appeared in the walls and though the disaster that seemed imminent never actually happened, the place became thoroughly unsafe. It is true, as I have said, that the place reverberated in the Thirties to the sound of the military bands but the days of gaiety were past. It was all very sad for those who had an inkling of the grander, more spacious days. Then, just after the 1939–45 war, the castle was pulled down and a few bungalows built from the stones. Days of penury also visited the Ravensworths who now live modestly many miles away.

Nowadays, as I have said, it is difficult indeed, to find the castle remains. Lady Park Lodge, now flanked by a group of modest semi-detached houses and within sight of a motorway, is at last traced. So is south lodge where there are forbidding signs which say respectively, "Keep out", "No road" and "Trespassers will be prosecuted". But in due course, driving up the 'No road', ignoring suspicious glances from the lush bungalows, and negotiating forest roads that seem to lead nowhere, I came at last to a glade at the side of which was a farm for young pheasants. Just ahead was the undergrowth and the two ruined towers. This journey was over except for one small, though crucial confirmation. I had also been looking for the tiny hamlet of Ravensworth, and there remains evidence, though only of the slightest, confirming that it was pulled down to allow the castle to be rebuilt. I doubt, though, if any castle, anywhere, could have had as short a reign as this one. But why do they seem nowadays to ignore the fact that it ever existed?

Close enough to Lamesley, and to Ravensworth Castle, too, is Kibblesworth which contains greater evidence of its deep rural past than of the colliery village it still was until recent times. A pleasant Plough Inn, snatches of green, old miners talking, eyes averted from a horribly vandalized shelter.

But a splendid green pleasance among the gravestones at the parish church, and a marvellous view across Kibblesworth Common, though you are high enough here to alter your gaze and see the fell across the valley, and where the quiet Team flowed slightly (and still flows) among the factories and the motorway.

There is the same suggestion of contrasts at Pelton: amid the betting shops and the bingo, a flavour of rural peace. Something the same at West Pelton and Beamish, but in the maze of byways around High Urpeth it is all quiet and high hedge—all, that is, until Birtley is reached.

Birtley has been a considerable village for several centuries. One hundred years ago it was on the main turnpike road to Durham, had shops, a post office, a police station and public houses galore. It is a considerable village still, and it seems to me, bears an unenviable reputation. It must be the noise capital of the North. I have seldom walked a main street to the accompaniment of such a traffic roar. Birtley bears the considerable disadvantage of being on the main road, not only from the factories of the Team Valley south, but from its own factories which are considerable and add an extra quota of heavy lorry menace to a road which, in any case, is far too narrow. I spent half a morning there, admiring the conversion of common land to golf course, the futuristic swimming pool, and the profusion of car parks. There were some things to deplore, but nothing worse than the conveyor belt of cars and lorries crashing their way south. I left Birtley behind me—I must confess thankfully—and it was now time to tackle The Fell.

In the beginning—or at any rate a few centuries ago—the bare fell rose high from the valley of the Team and then turned precipitously downward toward the Tyne. Before the Industrial Revolution, before coal, the hamlets which dotted the sides of the fell existed in conditions of considerable isolation. They were the refuge, at times, of eighteenth-century eccentrics, of highwaymen who plied the turnpike road below, of footpads, deserters from the fight against Napoleon—and all the roaming participants of the trades of the times. The parish of Gateshead Fell which adjoined Lamesley to the west and Heworth to the east, was, according to a contemporary writing at the end of the eighteenth century, composed of the villages of Sheriff Hill, Carr's Hill, Low Fell, Chowdean and Wrekenton. It was also, as I have indicated, a pretty unprepossessing, not to say wild locality for "it was studded with miserable mud huts and cottages, occupied by tinkers, cloggers, besom makers, egglers, muggers and others of the race called faws—these being itinerant workers of the lowest social pretension." A little order was imposed upon the chaos of these people by a Parliamentary Act of 1809 empowering the provision of roads and drains and other essential services. But order was slow in coming, and at Wrekenton in 1847 and again in 1849 the most frightful plague and pestilence was visited upon an exceedingly motley population. Wrekenton—in those days divided from the adjoining hamlet of Eighton Banks by a dyke—was such an odiferous place that consciences were stirred even in those unenlightened days and an enquiry ordered. The whole village, virtually, was condemned as being ill constructed, overcrowded, without ventilation, damp, dirty, with most of the houses having direct openings into ash pits. Small wonder, then, that Mr Francis Bennett, who conducted the enquiry, had to paint a distressing picture of the Wrekenton life style. This was worse—but not perhaps dramatically worse—than that being lived all over the Fell territory.

The troubles of Wrekenton began in 1847 with the outbreak of yellow fever, and when cholera struck two years later it carried off one seventh of the entire population within sixteen days in September. In some houses everyone died; specifically 110 died in an area of 158 houses. These gimcrack dwellings—hovels would be a much better word—had been pushed up at the turn of the century to house the pitmen working in the drift mines and the bell pits which almost surrounded the area. But the pits soon enough became worked out, the pitmen moved on, and their cottages had other occupants.

"The village," exclaimed a horrified inspector, "became the headquarters for all the vagrants in the district; men, women and children, with donkeys, pigs and dogs, all crowded in the same room; demoralization, filth and crime abounded." It was against this background that the cholera struck. Most of the hovels were pulled down, and the tinkers and tramps and their scrofulous families expelled, and Wrekenton became what was normal for The Fell.

They were a hard-boozing race of people, the number of public houses and beer shops defying present-day conception. Thus, five public houses and beer shops thrived at the village of Sheriff Hill nearby, where there seems to have been little else except a few workmen's cottages, the inevitable chapel of the Primitive Methodists and a lunatic asylum, while at Felling Shore, a village which does not exist today, and was small enough even then, six public houses prospered. At High Felling, just on the edge of the Fell district, the classic early nineteenth-century situation of beer and God could nowhere be more clearly exemplified. Then High Felling was a distant village on a lofty pinnacle; now it is indistinguishable from the urban sprawl which comes over the hill top towards both Team and Tyne. Then its population was composed of pitmen, quarry workers, and a profusion of service people. In most of them fear of God and liking of the liquor was nicely disseminated.

Thus there was in High Felling and in the even smaller hamlet of Low Felling a recently opened Roman Catholic church, and all the diffuse and mysterious breakaways of the Methodist church: The Independents, Methodist New Connection, Primitive Methodists, Wesleyan and Wesleyan Reformers. There were also fourteen public houses and eight beer shops, and Hogarthian scenes were enacted at all times of affluence which was when a few pence were available for gin, and when the children as well as the women were as likely to be drunk as the men—situations which in the later years of Victoria's reign were to bring forth the crusaders of the Salvation Army, and a few muscular Christians from the Church of England.

Meanwhile Low Fell was burgeoning as a large village with a dawning middle class, the few prosperous villas being built by the side of the new turnpike road to Durham. A little further on the Durham road was the hamlet of Chowdean. It is a fitting indication of the social pretension of both these places and the privilege they enjoyed that they became the first places—in 1857—in the whole Fell area to be lighted by gas.

The picture which emerges and which, indeed, was to persist until almost the turn of the present century was of isolated villages and hamlets up and over the side of the fell with raw countryside in between across which, in winter, the wind whistled and the snow settled, sometimes for weeks on end. Toil was sometimes stupefying; the death rate even without pestilence was appalling, but characters rose above their surroundings. Often they were earnest seekers after education, and like the early miners of the Durham coalfield, they achieved prodigies of knowledge. The fashion of poetasting which, as we have seen, was prevalent enough in rural nineteenth-century Teesdale was practised in the villages of the Fell. Events regularly were celebrated in verse, and then read out loud since aside from the few gentry at Low Fell hardly anyone could read.

One such, and typical of a small but hardy and dynamic breed, was Thomas Wilson who became not only a poet but a mathematician and merchant in Gateshead. Ironically though, he is remembered not for his multitudinous good works, but for what he liked to describe as his poetical compositions which—facile though they were—reflected the life and times of the working men which otherwise would have been unrecorded. His *Reflections on The Pitman's Pay Night* describing the mass trek to the public house is genuine social history, and the habit of all poetasters of the time to celebrate some obscure civic development is evinced in his stanzas on the intended new line of road from Potticar Lane to Leyburn Hole. Works like this and *The Oiling of Dickie's Wig* were read in public houses and in public places to the illiterate and were raucously enjoyed.

Thus the villages of the fell remained through the dawning of the Industrial Revolution. It was not really until the turn of the present century that massive building took place on the fellside, that Wrekenton and Eighton Banks merged imperceptively to High Fell—and High Fell into Low Fell.

And so the process went on, so that a problem indeed was presented when I went in search of what might remain of the villages of the fell today. In truth nothing very much does. It is useless, for example, looking for Sheriff Hill, though a native will point out to you where it once was, and the long rural walk (where you might be set on by tramps) between the south of Gateshead and the first cottages of the village. Wrekenton and Eighton Banks now are one, though vague distinguishing signs are said to exist. The place perched on the peak of the fell still has the cooling— not to say freezing—breezes, and all the signs of urban dross and dereliction coupled with some fine new houses, and old colliery cottages expensively refurbished.

From this promontory it is an easy step—say half an hour's

The ferryboat converted into a restaurant at Felling Shore

Wrekenton, a pit village last century

Eighton Banks, now merged with Wrekenton

Shincliffe, a desirable village to live in

Brancepeth village

Brancepeth Castle, empty since 1973

Stephenson's *Locomotion* No. 1 (*below*) Beamish Museum

Shotley Bridge, a quiet village of grey stone

Rookhope, one of the remotest places in Weardale

Elwick

Ebchester Church set in a village of the Derwent valley

Escomb Church, with its twelfth-century porch

A quarry landscape outside Stanhope

Stanhope Castle, now an approved school

Weardale. Stanhope in the distance, neat drystone walls in the foreground

walk—along the busy urban road to Windy Nook which again is indistinguishable from its surroundings. The road begins to cascade downwards to the Fellings. There is a place here called Windy Ridge where you can lean almost horizontally against the prevailing breezes. Here, surrounded by a mass of council housing, with highly imaginative graffiti on almost every surface in sight, there is the only remaining stretch of the naked hillside as it was more than a hundred years ago. This is about the size of half a dozen football pitches and is now known precisely as the Green.

Downwards still towards the Tyne, High Felling and Low Felling are simply part of the proliferation of urban Tyneside, though it is easy enough to imagine the forests on the fellside here, and the felling of the trees which gave the district its name. The final part of the descent takes one to Felling Shore where the village has long since disappeared under the heel of industry. So have all those pubs and beer shops. Some redundant industrial areas have been grassed and cultivated and made into an attractive riverside park where the Tyne, pungent when the tide is out and the sun shines, is by way of becoming a yachting centre. The ruin of an early Victorian schoolroom in what was presumably the centre of Felling Shore, has been allowed to persist in the middle of one of those grassy swards as what the planners hopefully regarded as an artistic focal point. Typically, perhaps, when I last was there it was so covered in chalky graffiti, tribal signs of the young citizenry, as to have a weird (and thoroughly noxious) design of its own.

There remains only that most prosperous part of The Fell which nowadays takes in both High Fell and Low Fell and is known by the latter name, Low Fell. It is parted neatly by the A1 which becomes the A1(M) a mile or so south. Within fifty years the fellside has been smothered in roads and avenues of villas which are solid, middle-class and prosperous and one cannot imagine—even though it was 150 years ago—any part of it being inhabited by tinkers, cloggers and besom makers as, of course, we know it was. There are plenty of vantage points where one can still gaze down upon the valley of the Team. The view is roughly the same as that I achieved at the other side at the beginning of this chapter which is of a trading estate, fifty factories and a motorway where once only the quiet Team flowed. But at least with this final view I can put a sight on (even if I cannot see) the secret places where Ravensworth Castle once stood.

It dawns, though, having written all this about an area which

F

(I do not believe) has ever been written about before, that I have not explained my reference in my opening paragraph to White Mere Pool. This, in fact, was formerly a hamlet maybe a couple of miles inland and eastward from Felling Shore, though I can never remember more than a couple of pubs there. There is recurring the impression that the White Mere should really be White Mare, and it is so described on some maps. In fact it derives its name from levels of stagnant water which has been tinged by the adjacent limestone and has nothing whatever to do with horses.

8

Around Durham City

THE perils of overcrowded classrooms are not, it would seem, a relatively new phenomenon.

Mr Hazey, a schoolmaster at Shincliffe which nowadays might loosely be called the village of academics on the outskirts of Durham City, is on record as complaining in the 1850s that "with classes of 140 it is impossible to keep order. The hot weather and the full school are beginning to tell on my health. I fear a break-down. . . ."

I mention this apparently inconsequential fact to illustrate that the quiet and exclusivity of Shincliffe which are now almost a way of life, are not necessarily permanent and certainly are not old. Shincliffe, in fact, is in the third of its phases in the Seventies. First, and for centuries, there was the agrarian. Then for several decades of the nineteenth century, and spurred on by coal and the coming of the railway, there was the tumult and the crowds which resulted (among many other things) in the incipient hysteria of Mr Hazey. Now everything is benign and most things are lovely in the village which is desired intensely as a living place by the burgeoning population of professors and the like from the University of Durham, by architects and planners, by exalted chief officials in local government, and by lesser citizens as well. It could be that other phases await Shincliffe, though there is little sign of change as one turns off the petrol ridden A177 from Durham to Teesside and is enmeshed immediately in a different world.

Shincliffe village in 1975 is a testimony to the good taste and well-lined pockets of those who live there. From 'The Rose Tree' on the right it rises gently, tree-lined and with green swards on either side, past 'The Railway Tavern' until 'The Seven Stars' is reached. In this way, and meandering no more than 300 or 400 yards, it takes in an attractive array of houses, cottages, conversions, a village post office, two delectable small estates, a church, a hall, and a converted railway station.

There is a pleasantly jumbling effect of stone, brick, slate and pantile. When I was last there—on a Saturday morning in summer—boys were practising cricket in the middle of the village street, and three cars in half an hour skirted them without complaint. In the unlikely event of a house becoming available there is great competition from all the sorts of people just mentioned, and prices even in these inflationary times are calculated only to dismay the buyers.

Yet Shincliffe in the larger sense has two faces and, one suspects, two social strata. For across the A177 and ascending a short and steepish hill one comes to High Shincliffe, known to the locals as Bank Top. This was the site of most of the tumult. When Shincliffe Village, aside from an occasional member of the quality, was the place where farm labourers lived and worked the Bank Top was full of excitement and excess, for up there on the plateau they found coal.

In 1837 they began sinking the shaft for Shincliffe Colliery and a whole new town quickly came into being. This was the end of the quietude of centuries. Itinerant miners and their families poured in from other places, and to house them they built Single Row, Shop Row, Pit Row, Double Row, Chapel Row and Back Row, not to mention Quality Street where the higher officials lived with their families and servants. By 1851 there were 134 such homes, and by 1872 there were 280 miners belonging to the Shincliffe Colliery Lodge.

Therefore the surprising explosion in village education, though attendances did not always attain the peak which so perplexed Mr Hazey. When trade was bad the miners simply refused to pay the 3d to 6d a week school fee, 'and classes diminished sharply when pecuniary or even amusing diversions competed for attention. Thus "children absent to watch a man hung" is a report in March 1865.

In those days you had to be ten years old to work down the pit, but one schoolmaster wearily reported a succession of parents seeking witness from him that their children, younger than that, could read and write and were therefore competent to leave and earn a living underground.

One of the colliery owners of the time was the idyllically named Mr Love who also had one of the rows of pit houses named after him. He gave thousands of pounds to the Methodist church, but Edward Welbourne writing in his history of the Miners Union of Northumberland and Durham gives also a different side to his character. Apparently he made £5,000 a year from fining miners who did not fill their coal baskets to the brim. He stopped credit at the shops he owned when his miners went on strike, evicted men, women and children from their homes and practised a vicious form of nepotism which denied all promotion except to his relatives and friends. Shincliffe Pit closed in 1875, one of the many at that time where the coal simply ran out. There had been no time, really, to form a pit community which, as we have seen, welded other Durham villages together over the generations. So the story at Shincliffe was not of solidarity but division, not endurance but dissolution. Most of the miners moved on to the other, more recently sunken pits where coal was in good supply. And as they did so, the brief industrial resurgence of Shincliffe began to ebb away, for though other industries also had sprung up they lacked resilience and indeed, a reason now for their existence, and in due time the brick works, the saw mill, the bottle works simply faded away.

In the meantime down the bank the village had undergone a simpler and much quieter revolution caused by the coming of the railway. It came from Sunderland, and opened up at the bottom of the village in 1839 and was regarded with so much apparent indifference by the inhabitants that the Durham *Advertiser* observed only: "We understand that the railway line . . . has opened at Shincliffe Station last week."

In the event the railway remained there until 1893, but The Railway Tavern, as I can testify, still thrives.

At this time there was tacit recognition that Shincliffe was really two communities, and when the census of 1851 was held the population at Bank Top was quite separately assessed. Viewing the village as a whole, though, the coming of the miners had brought about a huge population explosion. The number of people, 282 in 1811, was 1,175 by 1851 and 2,000 at the peak of activity in 1870. But while Bank Top was undergoing the painful spasms of the early Industrial Revolution, the village, despite the railway, remained virtually unchanged. A few miners, it is true, lived there; but the number was only thirty. For the rest, it remained a tight little agricultural community, with the large number of incidental service people that so puzzles us today. Four shoemakers, two tailors, five dressmakers, seven public houses—and a brewery of which local historian John Stredwick has been unable to find any trace today.

With the pit closure the way was clear for another remarkable revolution, and this was the wiping out over several decades of virtually every trace of industrial activity on the Bank Top so that now you can tour the pleasant houses of the new estates and scarcely be aware that such activity ever existed. The miners, as we have said, moved on; their houses were sold for £10 each and there were few takers at the price. Some aged miners perforce, stayed; then they died and their houses fell into ruins. By 1894 Bank Top was deserted; by 1920 half of it was pulled down; by 1946 the demolition was complete. The colliery buildings went; neat detached houses stand on the sites of both pit heaps. Even the racecourse which prospered fitfully from 1895 (5,500 crowded through the shilling turnstiles at one meeting) could not survive the depression which came after the 1914–18 war. Nowadays only the grandstand remains and that is used as a barn. Meanwhile the village progressed gradually towards exclusiveness.

The few miners' cottages were pulled down; then the railway station closed upon the completion of the line through old Durham to Elvet station. But right up to the 1930s the main road had run round sharp bends through the village. Then a beauty spot known as the back lane was gouged away to form a by-pass.

The demise of the old trades was at a speed as quick as anything seen in other villages. Only the blacksmith remained until the early 1930s. As the years went by the village increased in beauty. The line of trees, planted in about 1900 now give it the intense country character and adds to the wonderful somnolence of a summer afternoon. The village post office and shop remains, thankfully unmodernized, and where old cottages have been developed, this has been accomplished with unassuming good taste.

Shincliffe is élitist and delectable. I hope it is only imagination which conveys an impression, sometimes almost overpowering, of some sort of silent presence willing you to go away.

If Shincliffe neglects to hold out an hilarious welcome (and why should it?) then neither, it must be said, does Brancepeth. This is likewise a very pleasant place, a few miles away on the A690 from Durham to Crook, but resembles Shincliffe in no other way. For here there is massive castle, parkland, church, championship golf course, so that the village, such as it is, is almost submerged in grandeur. To arrive at Brancepeth on a summer morning with the sun pouring down on the sleek fairways, the

guard dogs baying as one presses the castle bell, the stonemasons
at work in the churchyard, and the meadow grasses flowing in the
breeze, is to be diverted from thought of the village which, indeed, is so unassuming as scarcely to be noticed. But there is a
profound irony in the current relationship between castle and
village, the one so desirable, the other which—seemingly—no one
wants.

The golf course one must take for granted; the church, a pleasant amalgam of the twelfth, thirteenth and fourteenth centuries,
is gorgeously situated so that it seems impossible to imagine the
pitmatic blight of Meadowfield, Langley Moor and Brandon and
Byshottles only a couple of miles away. Someone had a good idea
of picking out the human points in this church in leaflet form so
that the ill-tutored or ignorant do not have to wander about
hazily, as one does in strange churches, searching the walls and the
tablets and the effigies for something to take one's fancy. Here all
is simplicity: twelve points to notice inside and six out, and even
for someone like myself for whom church architecture provokes
only a dazed and neurotic inattention, the information is conveyed with simplicity and humour. Thus: "Of those vast effigies
in the chancel, Robert Nevill, who lived in the fourteenth century
and is better known as 'The Peacock of the North' is the one in
stone. He was always fighting someone—he slew a fellow noble-
man on the Framwellgate bridge at Durham and was himself slain
at Berwick in 1319. By his head you can just make out the backs
of the chantry priests praying for his soul. Perhaps he needed
their prayers!"

The font is of Frosterley marble, Frosterley being only a few
miles away since Brancepeth is virtually at the gateway to Weardale. Most interesting to me, though, and something I had seen
nowhere else (the fault being mine, maybe, since I tend to give
churches cursory glances unless persuaded otherwise) was the
diagram of the pews. This had been done in 1639 and had great
detail showing the actual names of the occupants of the pews,
with the men and the women worshipping separately. On the outside there is a stone stile made of medieval gravestones and also
an iron grating to keep out the animals. This last supports an
interesting historical point which is that long ago the village came
right up to the church walls. Parts of the foundations of old
cottages are still dug up on occasion in the churchyard. Now the
village ends at least 200 yards away.

Fifty yards away is the extraordinary castle, a considerable circle of stone. No crumbling medieval edifice this. It is, by contrast, immensely strong, imposing—and useless. We will be writing about the Rising of the North and the part played at Raby. But at Brancepeth, also then owned by the Nevills, they had the army headquarters. It was here, reckoned to be stronger than Raby and the oldest fortified castle in the realm, that the important people scheming for the liberation of Mary Queen of Scots foregathered. It was of the situation at Brancepeth that Wordsworth has written:

> From every side came noisy swarms,
> Of peasants in their homely gear;
> And, mixed with these, to Brancepeth came
> Grave gentry of estate and name.

But as at Raby, so of course at Brancepeth. The gentry and the peasants seem to have been extraordinarily ill prepared. Their ultimatum to Queen Elizabeth was received with a frosty determination that they should be crushed and, since the only artillery they possessed was three small brass pieces, the Queen's men were not resisted and the rebels simply faded away.

Thus Brancepeth like Raby was forfeited to the Crown, but after that similarity being noted, the history of these places could not have been more different. Raby, as we will see belonged only to the Vanes; Brancepeth moved from owner to owner. Raby was (and is) cherished and, as a result, a kind and intimate relationship grew up between castle and village. Brancepeth has had money heaped upon its walls to gratify eighteenth-century conceit, but there was precious little identification with village or people. Raby lived; Brancepeth existed.

Brancepeth was given by James I to the notorious Robert Ker, Earl of Somerset, who himself had it forcibly taken from him for allegedly poisoning Sir Thomas Overbury. Always it seems, Brancepeth Castle has been available. William Russell, the Sunderland tycoon, bought it in 1796 and he and his son Matthew, the richest commoner in England, were responsible for its great resuscitation. They spent £120,000 in rebuilding the interior, destroyed much of the ancient fabric, gave it a drab but lasting ordinariness inside, and even eliminated its secrets.

In 1922 it became the headquarters of the Durham Light Infantry and in the late 1960s seemed at last to achieve some sort of relevancy to the present when it became the Advanced Research Laboratory for a glass manufacturer. But since 1973 the castle has

been empty again. It has 240 rooms, and has an oak door, presumably leading to a dungeon, which has not been opened in
living memory. But who wants 240 rooms these days? When I
last visited Brancepeth the rumours were wild, topical and seemed
motivated by wish fulfilment. Mr Telly Savalas, the *Kojak* folk
hero of American and British television, was said to have visited
Brancepeth in a white Mercedes (in fact he was in Berlin). An oil
sheik was going to buy the place. But as I write, no one has. It is
a castle that might inspire both Wordsworth and Tennyson (who
wrote *Maud* during a visit there). But who will buy it today?

But I spoke of an irony and it is this: that in 1975 the tiny
village, so oppressed apparently, and rendered self-effacing by the
grandeur of the castle is itself nowadays desirable, whereas the
castle is merely a massive blight on the property market. The few
period cottages which, in effect, form a driveway to the castle
gates are highly individual, and their situation is so delectable,
nestling away from the thundering traffic on the A690, that they
have become highly prized. If Magnolia Cottage, for example, were
to come on the market for £20,000 the affluent would beat a path
to its door. Further away, across the main road in the direction
of where Brancepeth station used to be, the magic of the name,
and the aura, maybe, of the castle nobody wants to buy still persists, and splendid houses are quickly built and sold. It is very nice,
in fact, to have a Brancepeth address as long as it is not Brancepeth Castle.

From Brancepeth I made my way by devious secondary roads to
Aycliffe, Middridge and Heighington, the round-about route being
necessary in order to avoid the towns of Crook and Willington,
while at the same time skirting both Bishop Auckland and Shildon,
towns also of a heavily pitmatic influence. Hereabouts every way
seems to turn to a pit town or village that was, the pits, of
course, having all been closed for some years. Every road, also
seems to be attracted, almost magnetically towards the A1(M)
which is slashing its way southward, or alternatively towards the
old A1 now masquerading as the A167. The purpose was to see
how those villages—all equidistant from the new town of Newton
Aycliffe were existing under what was presumed to be its shadow.
I had not forgotten the relatively unhappy experience of the old
village of Washington under the tutelage of Washington New
Town. Had this experience been repeated?

In the event what has transpired at Aycliffe, Heighington and at
the hamlet of Middridge is quite different and for two reasons. The

first is that whereas the old village of Washington is part of the new town and therefore subject to its edicts and its influence, the villages I have mentioned are quite separate from Newton Aycliffe despite their proximity. In addition Newton Aycliffe is much the oldest new town in Durham, having being in the act of creation and evolution since 1947. It has thus had ample time to develop a corporate personality and community spirit of its own, and to have largely rid itself of the new town blues—a condition caused by a great proliferation of housing either in garden city or neighbourhood concept—but scarcely any amenity for leisure or pleasure. Newton Aycliffe, where there are schools and clubs and pubs of every description, where vandalism is surprisingly meagre, and where the new town experience may cautiously be said to be succeeding, had presumably sent out tentacles of influence to the smaller fry on its doorstep. But now that the life style gives satisfaction, that influence, on the whole, is benign. There is also none of the newness of the new town residents and that feeling of being uprooted from other, older districts which causes trouble in other parts. The people largely are second generation, or have moved in from the villages mentioned. The links, then, such as they are between the brash and growing new town and the old villages, are good.

At Middridge which is within new town control the experience has been totally beneficial. Middridge was a doomed colliery hamlet and in really a terrible state of dereliction when in the later 1960s, it was decided—not only that Newton Aycliffe should be expanded, but that Middridge should be resuscitated within its orbit. This has been successfully, indeed triumphantly, achieved by retaining the village frontage to the houses, by cherishing the village green, and by ensuring that the shop, the post office and the pub were not out of keeping with the general design.

At both Aycliffe and Heighington, however, there is no overt sign of new town influence. Heighington, pleasantly split by the main road from Bishop Auckland to Darlington, has segmented greens, a jumbled architecture, with a few fine regency survivals and much solid Victorian worth. The pubs are ordinary, and it is not the sort of village that might house an antique shop of distinction. Nowadays it is surrounded by flowing fields, by dairy and crop farming, and the pace is somewhat slow. But Heighington, which is not well known even within the boundaries of Durham, and could even be characterized as remote and unpretentious, has two somewhat surprising historical associations which occurred within twenty years of each other. It was involved with the first passenger railway train and also, however vicariously, with the Battle of Trafalgar.

The railway association is somewhat fortuitous. The engine *Locomotion No. 1* was built by George Stephenson for the Darlington and Stockton Railway and brought down from Newcastle in pieces in horse-drawn carts. Then it was reassembled and placed on the line at Heighington Level. Thereupon, on 27th September 1825 it drew 450 passengers and six wagons of coal on the first public passenger service from Darlington to Stockton: the first in the world.

There seems to have been a chance, however remote, that Heighington that day might have witnessed a tragedy, for it seems that the boiler of *Locomotion No. 1* was intolerably weak—even by the standards of the day—and was in danger of bursting. In the event it did burst but not until 1828 when it was standing harmlessly at a nearby junction. However it was rebuilt and served in various capacities until 1857. Heighington is very proud of this association, but if one wants to be unduly pernickety it could be pointed out that the level where everything happened is in fact situated in the adjoining parish of Aycliffe. So far as Trafalgar is concerned, however, the honour belongs to Heighington alone.

The family involved—the Cumbys—have lived in Heighington for 250 years and in recent times have changed the name to Cumby Spurrier. The hero of whom Heighington is so proud was Captain Wm. Bryce Cumby who entered the Battle of Trafalgar as second in command of HMS *Bellerophon*. His captain was killed: Cumby took over, sank a French ship and in due course came back to Heighington in triumph where he built a large house, named it after the battle, and became a worthy of the neighbourhood. There is much more to his life; much, too, of the fascinating impedimenta of his career in Bowes Museum at Barnard Castle, and a great, great-grandson named Horatio after Lord Nelson, is still in the village as I write.

A couple of miles away (you pass Heighington Level on the way) Aycliffe village sits astride the old A1 and at first glance is very unprepossessing indeed. Traffic rushes through continually: to stand at the roadside is to be enveloped in a noxious cloud, and the noise is unrelenting. This is the vision of the speedy traveller, but turn off the main road and there is a remarkable transformation. The village green is the neatest I have seen anywhere, and new houses of distinctive design are grouped in nice little causeways and even the pubs are friendly. The village was proudly brandishing its trophy as winner of the county Tidy Village competition when I was there—and never an honour, it would seem, had been more deservedly won.

There was not a scrap of paper, an errant leaf, even a matchstick to be seen. No compulsion is (or indeed could be) enforced to keep the paper from the streets, the grass cut, the gardens as though each house was inhabited by a race of magical gardeners. Pride accelerates the village ambition: the point of honour becomes so ingrained that even a schoolchild does not throw away a toffee paper. It looks to be the village of a happy obsession.

When I began the series of journeys that are encompassed in this chapter, the intention was to insinuate myself into a group of villages within sight almost of the cathedral in Durham city. So much for vain intention. Shincliffe fell easily into that role, and through Brancepeth, in a literal sense has no such vision, it is near enough to the Neville's Cross junction properly to be included in the arrangement. With Aycliffe and Heighington one was led sadly astray by some sort of compulsive peccadillo. For though the destinations would have had to be attained—perhaps in some other chapter—the attainment came about in the manner described rather because, once Brancepeth had been visited, certain immediate fascinations lay in view. The first was that to travel by the side of Brancepeth golf course on a shining June morning was a journey full of sparkling delight across the Wear, with the happy surprise of approaching Spennymoor, a scarred and forgettable colliery town, by a tree-lined pleasance that could easily have graced a village entrance in Sussex or Hampshire.

The second was the desire, which dawned only as the journey had begun, to look at places which previously were only names on a map or notoriously, maybe, in a newspaper. Thus, across the crossroads at which there are no signposts and Kirkmerrington is reached, and Page Bank and Old Eldon and Tottenham—Tottenham?—and Redworth. One led to the other, and in each, or almost in all, the evidence is there of rurality and decaying pitmatic presence. The wonder all the time is that perhaps nature which was rudely pushed aside by the Industrial Revolution may assert herself again.

The signs are there that it is about to happen and that within a hundred years or so, the green swards may clothe the land again. It was this sort of beguilement, anyway, which led me on almost in spite of myself to Heighington and Aycliffe. It was a similar sort of journey—the last it was my intention to take around Durham City—that concluded with the fascinating story of a victory by nature in a village which—I freely confess—I had never heard of before and alighted upon by the purest accident.

I thought I would inspect Sherburn, was unhappy with what I saw, pushed on, and thus, on a crowded, noisy, shopping Saturday morning, drove quickly through Coxhoe into a place called Quarrington Hill. From here I became strangely lost in an isolation of small hills and sweeping pasture in the parish (so the church notice board at the top of a hill informed me) of Cassop-cum-Quarrington with Bowburn. Along this rolling road there was a quarry in the distance with a mass of white flowers on top, an area of what seemed to be thinly disguised industrial dross at the roadside similarly adorned and, as I proceeded, notices announcing that this was a conservation area. Yet this was no national park; there were demonstrably no buildings of special importance. This was, to be explicit, an old area of the Durham coalfield now largely worked out, narrowly fitting into a wedge bounded on the west side by the A177 and to the east by the A19. Although the white flowers were pretty enough and, within the context of their situation a little unusual, there did not, at first sight, seem anything as far as the horizon (and it was a day of shimmering heat and blue, enticing distances) that remotely required to be conserved.

But plainly this was not the case. I spoke to a man exercising alsatians, then the vicar, and was directed in due course (but not without considerable mischance) to the good offices of Mr Nixon who lived at the School House at Cassop. It was he who quietly, gravely, courteously, with books in his study and with excursions in the field, elucidated the mystery of Cassop Vale—for this, indeed, was the area I had chanced upon.

Cassop Vale is approximately in the centre of the three parishes of Kelloe, Coxhoe and Cassop-cum-Quarrington. It would be an exaggeration to say that these parishes are distinctly divided; indeed in the centre of the inconsiderable village of Quarrington Hill, all three intermingle mysteriously with each other. Thus you can visit the chapel in Cassop, turn the corner to get your hair cut in the parish of Kelloe, and have a pint at the pub across the street in Coxhoe.

Cassop Vale, at the back of the village street falls away on either side of the road, passes a pub ('The Heather Lad') which has no running water, and then swings to the right through a stretch of scrub and gorse to old Cassop and then to Cassop Colliery. It was this village wherein dwelt Mr Nixon near the school over which he presided for so many years, and from which our foray of enlightenment set forth.

An escarpment ran through the vale six hundred feet high, and at the foot, in the deep and green shadows eight collieries were sunk about 140 years ago. They were Kelloe Winning, South Kelloe, Crowtrees, Old Coxhoe, Heughall, Cassop Moor, Cassop Vale and Cassop.

By the standards of the pits we have described elsewhere they were tiny, and were not destined for any acrimonious or dramatic life. No great tragedies occurred; no confrontations between embryo trade unions and hard-faced bosses. Most were reasonably productive for a few decades, and then, sometime in the 1860s, they began to run out of coal. By the early 1890s, it is safe to say that all were ended. There is no one in Cassop today who can remember any of them in production. So that, from about 1865 onwards, life in the vale began to die away. The pits grew silent, the pit buildings became deserted; the limestone pit houses first became disused, then tumbled down, and the stone was either carted away or allowed to retreat into the limestone background from which it had come. The spoil heaps were naturally reclaimed by the self-sowing of hawthorn, hazel, gorse, broom and sycamore. The large natural pond in the centre of all this which had supplied water for the colliery engines, reverted to its ageless purpose, and the stream running straight through the vale again became undisturbed and the wild life returned. In all the decades since the last pit closed the area has been naturally conserved, for no one really went there, and this isolation, allied to the peculiar mix of natural resources has led to the nature fairyland of today. You have, in a reasonably restricted area upon and below the escarpment, the flora associated with limestone, clay, sandstone, woodland and marsh. In a deep area of marshy remoteness grew some of the rarest of orchids in the land. Everywhere there are hosts of white flowers, marigolds, foxglove, violet, anemone, bluebell, the rare oxlip. Rare marsh plants proliferate round pond and stream. If you must be statistical, then 146 different flowers have been found and duly documented. And though frogs are tending to disappear from those areas of the local countryside where ponds are being filled in and chemical fertilizers in use, they thrive here as does stickleback, newt, and that comparative rarity—the toad.

There are, of course, foxes, badgers, stoats, weasels, the visiting heron and kingfisher, and it is all conserved by an understanding county council. When you stand on the peak of the escarpment and look right and left, and into the distances that are as beguiling as those on an Italian landscape, there is no sign of the tumult of the middle nineteenth century. There is no pithead or pithouse, nothing except one small engine room intruding from the distant undergrowth. It is symbolic, I suppose, of what has gone before, but in a few more years of rampant growth it will have disappeared completely.

9

Into North-west Durham

IT sometimes seems to the uninitiated that north-west Durham is compounded solely of pits, the excrescences they produce, the villages created to serve those pits, and the resulting tawdry environment when the pits die. In fact the area also has much natural beauty and not a little historical interest. Villages exist on the very fringe of the coalfield which owe little—if anything—to pitmatic influence. The further west one also goes, the higher the ground and the greater frequency of stark moorland. The winter snows persist on the heights above Lanchester, and the road thereafter to 'The Punchbowl' at Satley—where the steaks are luscious and the beer cool—can be direly afflicted with fog. Yet in the summer under a pristine sky, the air is sparkling, the silence pregnant, the occasional raven or buzzard wheels in the heavens, and there are rare wild orchids to be discovered—in the remote likelihood, that is, of one knowing where to look.

There is also never a pit in sight, either active or passive, dead or alive. The industrial emphasis changes to hill and moorland farming, and if one moves northward to the heights above Consett the vista is not of colliery, but of the ochre landscapes and gaunt chimneys that spell steel.

This is one section of Durham County which is stuffed with the evidence of the past. The registrars hereabouts have been assiduous, and the local historians concerned that a heritage should be placed on record. There is also, in the village of Beamish, a remarkable recent experiment which aims at the preservation of a vanished age. It is, all in all, a piece of the county that is not only full of surprises, but exudes a brisk optimism. The present is neither neurotic nor too self-critical; the future beckons with hope, in contrast, as we have seen to the dead pit lands of Quaking Houses where only the past has fascination.

In Whickham, therefore, which is the first of the villages I have in mind, Quaking Houses is light years away. A middle-class aura greets you. This, nowadays, is commuter country; it is an increasing dormitory for Newcastle, and this fact, plus the newness of much of the population, led to an experience on my first visit which brought more than a hint of desperation.

I was seeking a well-known address, the house of a retired headmaster in a cul-de-sac off one of the main thoroughfares. Where, then, was it? I stopped the car three times in Whickham Highway, which is the village main street. Each time I was courteously denied an explicit direction. A policeman in a panda car stopped, eager to please and when he could not give an answer ("I've only been here six months") radioed his HQ who were equally devoid of intelligence.

By now I was late, but at the post office the chief man, deploring that the postwoman was not there ("She would have known") sent me to the council offices, where an enquiry clerk was quick to suggest that I go elsewhere. But by now, feeling like a helpless denizen in an alien land, I grew stubborn, suggested forcibly to the clerk that it was incumbent upon him as the resident and most readily available official person to provide what seemed at that moment to be an almost impossible solution to my dilemma. He looked mutinous but a middle-aged lady passed, spotted the stricken look on my face, and promised that, with the efficiency of the people of Whickham on trial, she would find out the whereabouts of the elusive cul-de-sac I sought. A moment later she was back with the answer: the address—the houses had been there for forty years—was less than half a mile from where we stood.

I do not exaggerate all this, but it is inconceivable that such a dilemma would have presented itself in any of the pit villages where, when I looked lost or enquired a direction, the answer was usually instantaneous. In Whickham that sort of deep local identification, as in commuter territory everywhere, is simply absent, and as more and more new estates and houses are imposed upon the older village this situation becomes more pronounced.

Whickham, as they say, is a good postal address: a prestigious place in which to live, so that, if you have a certain turn of mind, you find it pleasant to put Whickham, Co. Durham at the head of your notepaper rather than Dunston which is the working-class suburb of Gateshead next door. A pleasant place, withal, with its quota of eighteenth-century cottages, fine houses of the early nineteenth century, and the vestige of a village green remaining outside the council offices. There is also a local controversy or two:

G

the sense or otherwise of plans for a new shopping centre, the plight of the communally minded at the dire lack of a decent community centre—and what to do with the vandals. These ought not to exist in a middle-class market place, but they do—the state of the public conveniences bore testimony to that. But perhaps, as conservative local opinion suggests—the vandals come in marauding bands from less seemly places like Swalwell which is a village close by of lesser pretensions.

There is an unusual bit of history about the green. In 1852 a person named Atkins laid claim to it largely, it seems, because of his occupancy of a house alongside it known as the old Post Office. He proceeded to cut down trees which grew along the churchyard wall, and then to dig a quarry in the middle of the green which he enclosed with wooden rails. Uproar in the village was intense. An effigy of Atkins was carried aloft, and his safety for a time was in some doubt. But it seems that Atkins had been careless. He was only the tenant of the house which, he claimed, gave him right to quarry the green. So the Rector, a wealthy Mr Carr, bought the house over his head, dispossessed the unseemly Atkins, and presented the green to the village "for ever". Somewhat cultivated and circumscribed, it is there to this day.

Whickham has never really been the haven of famous people, nor is it today. With Gibside Hall close by, though, the Bowes family have been much in evidence, including that unhappy heiress, the widowed Countess of Strathmore. Wesley preached in Whickham; Cromwell slept here, or hereabouts when, in 1650, he drove his armies to Scotland. An eighteenth-century Master of the King's Musick, William Shield, lived here but was buried in Westminster Abbey. Harry Clasper, a famous Victorian waterman of the Tyne who wrested the world's professional rowing championship from the experts of the Thames, is buried in Whickham churchyard.

Fame of this vicarious sort, however, has usually passed Whickham by, but no matter, there have always been those who sang its praises. William Hutchinson, perhaps the most famous of Durham's many historians, described the chief buildings (this was in 1787) as "modern and handsome" and the prospect from the south side as "remarkably beautiful". From this vantage point you could see the villages of Ryton, Benwell, Elswick, Newburn and Lemington, and the landscape was dotted with cottages, quarries and windmills.

When Napoleon threatened to invade England they raised a volunteer force of 500 at Whickham, and a local iron-founder made a strong chain which was intended to obstruct the passage of the Emperor's ships up the Tyne at night. The local church-wardens recorded a plague of foxes in the eighteenth century, and awarded a shilling for every head and 7½d for the head of each wild cat, which vanished animal seems to have been equally numerous. Inspection of their registers at this time records the expediture of fourpence for a chamber pott, and the slaughter of the dog population because of an epidemic of rabies.

From Whickham to Beamish it is a few twisted, urban miles on the Stanley Road. Beamish itself is inconsequential and has been briefly referred to previously. It was the home of the late Jack Lawson, profound Methodist, thinking politician, Labour Party scion and peer who had a brief period as War Minister under Attlee. Jack used to say that no one ever came to his humble village unless he brought them—but that was before the day when they decided to make it the site of an open-air museum which is developing with a decided originality and which has some aspects which are unique.

For many years there had been an awareness that not only Durham but the whole northern region was a fascinating repository of all the bits and pieces of social history especially as this applied from the beginning of the Industrial Revolution. There was also a fear that unless steps were taken to gather in and make safe items of vanishing work practices and styles of life they would simply disappear. It was decided, therefore, that though the first attempt had been made at Bowes Museum, Barnard Castle, to marshal a few appropriate exhibits, a completely new museum was necessary. This is what has been established in part of the old hall at Beam-ish by an amalgam of local authorities, and run by Frank Atkinson who is outstandingly the most knowledgeable social historian in the region. It is an astonishing place. Jack Lawson, if he were alive today, would have to amend his remarks about people avoid-ing his village. Though the museum has been there rather less than five years there were 140,000 visitors in the summer of 1974—and this with the museum still in an embryonic stage.

There are about 200 acres of undulating parkland and the exhibits are to be so arranged as to compose a living entity. The centre of a small town is to be created with cobbled street, market place, town hall, police and fire stations, and a variety of small shops, public house and even, in all probability, a 1930s Italian ice cream par-lour. There will be a builder's yard, a small town gas works, and various craftsmen's workshops. A lot of the buildings have already been acquired from various parts of the region, dismantled and stored ready for re-erection as part of the grand design. An old electric tramway system is to be created and one tramcar, a Gateshead No. 10 in service in Gateshead and Newcastle from 1925 until about 1950, has already been acquired and occasionally runs.

A colliery direct from the nineteenth century is to be created; there will be a vertical winding engine from the local colliery which was built in 1855. There is so much more, as well. Complete colliery cottages, farm workers' cottages, a blacksmith's shop, a railway station, *circa* 1867, four famous steam rollers, one of which, the Coquet Lass, was used in Rothbury, Northumberland from 1899. There are plans to preserve old prefab houses built just after the last war, as an exceedingly temporary measure. A few still remain, and next time a local authority announces plans for demolition of its remaining prefabs, there will be a request from Beamish that a row of them be handed over to them.

Museum authorities are perplexed these last few years for lack of money, their ambitious plans to spend up to £500,000 on new buildings and car parks understandably coming a good way down the priority list of local government cash allotments. In the meantime, though, they keep acquiring the massive impedimenta of the region roughly from 1870 onwards: everything from milk bottle tops in use before the age of plastic to children's hand-made shoes, and the type of plane used by the village carpenter in 1905. Books come to them by the hundred and thousand, books of the abstruse kind nobody else could conceivably want. If you are wondering, for example, where you may find the Plumbers Handbook for 1882 I can tell you that it fell from the sprawling, chaotic shelves at Beamish while I was browsing, lost in a dream of gas-lit streets, mutton chop whiskers, and ladies with bustle skirts and bonnets.

In this state I virtually tripped over another exhibit, certainly of the period: a painted wooden board containing a moralizing stanza in contemporary script about Mary Ann Cotton, the Victorian multiple murderer from West Auckland. This lady poisoned her numerous husbands and children, the reason, in so far as she had one, being the small amount of funeral money she received from the parish on each occasion:

> She murdered her husbands and lodger as well,
> The numbers she poisoned, no one can tell,
> So anxious she was for money 'tis said,
> That she ordered their coffins before they were dead.

The strong hand of justice compelled her to stay,
And her crimes have been proved as clear as the day.
Now in Durham Prison condemned she does lie,
And soon on the scaffold she will have to die.

Another of those villages which virtually hugs the Durham coal-fields yet is not remotely part of it, is Lanchester which can be reached from Beamish by skirting the town of Stanley, or more attractively, I think, by traversing the A691 from Durham. Lanchester presents itself as a single rural street with council housing cunningly hidden away. As the name obviously implies, there is the site, here, of a Roman fort. But all physical evidence of the fort has long since disappeared, so that the place—about 200 feet above the village on the road to Wolsingham—has to be pointed out. This is a bleak area about 600 feet above sea level, just about the line where the mists and snows linger. Watling Street, that ancient British highway, crossed the Lanchester–Wolsingham road at right angles about here, but there is no evidence of this either, nor, as one went about Lanchester on one of the days when the fog stole right into the village, much interest or knowledge either.

Still there is Roman evidence if you search assiduously enough. There is a Roman altar in the south porch of the magnificent old church, this came from Hurbeck Farm about a couple of miles from the main fort. Many of the stones of the fort were used in the building of local farms and some are certainly a part of the church tower. Ancient British remains, too, have been discovered and these included a sword, scythes and four axe heads.

The modern village is somewhat pessimistically inclined, the old people harking back, as most old people will, to vanished glories—or maybe, more accurately to a serenity which is lost. The young complain, with some justice, that there is nothing to do; nothing, that is, if you are seeking town pleasures. Much of the overt picturesqueness disappeared from the village with the driving through of the Durham–Consett road. The green had to be reduced and two hump-backed bridges removed. Now, with the loss of some individuality the traffic at least flows freely; before, it coagulated and could bring village life to a virtual standstill, particularly on mart days. Now there is no mart either, nor is there a railway station or a yearly point-to-point, or even a police court with cells attached. Still, pessimistic or not, the place exudes prosperity—one sure indication being a gorgeous antique shop which the Americans, the Dutch and the Germans find unerringly.

Up the hill on the Wolsingham road, past the site of the Roman

fort and where the road levels out at the hamlet of Hollinside is
Colepike Hall, a thirty-two-room mansion, which the owner, Tom
Bellord, shares with a friend, June Hulbert and her husband and
family. It was here that that notorious rascal, Andrew Robinson
Stoney, first impinged on the awareness of northern life in the
eighteenth century. He was an impecunious half-pay Naval lieuten-
ant when he met Miss Hannah Newton, an heiress with money—
about £20,000 of it—derived from the Newcastle coal trade, as
well as the Colepike property. Stoney possessed an attractive Irish
charm—attractive when he exerted himself—which was unfailingly
when intent on shady deeds.

He saw in Miss Newton a first step towards affluence and duly
married the shy country girl. Soon—and predictably—she was
desperately unhappy. First he undermined what self-confidence she
possessed by subtly provoking her in company, and then, when she
looked displeased, appealing that his cause was just and unfailingly making her seem at fault. His poor wife gave birth to a
succession of still-born children and this increasingly infuriated
Stoney as being some commentary—his curious mental processes
suggested—on his own virility. Thus he caused the bells of Lanchester Church to be rung, indicating that the births had been
live. Subsequently he is said to have pushed her down a flight of
stairs, and then for varying periods locked her in a closet with, it
is said, a single egg as her sole daily sustenance and clad only in a
chemise. Thankfully the poor lady quickly died, which one is persuaded was always the aim of Stoney. He succeeded to her property and after a brief interval of grotesque mourning he was available for his next adventure in which he married, and quickly drove
frantic, the unhappy Mary Eleanor Bowes, Countess of Strathmore.
Thus Stoney became associated with Gibside, near Whickham
which we have already referred to. His subsequent career was
notorious but has nothing more to do with Lanchester.

Ebchester is another of those villages which has successfully
resisted being engulfed by the coalfield, though the influences are
perilously near. It is some little distance away on another road
to Consett, and is altogether quieter. Indeed, I have never been in
Ebchester when it has not seemed deserted. This, presumably, is
ascribable to the fact that there is no centre for the surrounding
countryside as there is at Lanchester; farmers do not foregather
here; there is no gathering of the country clans at bank or teashop
or supermarket. It is the site of another Roman station, though in
this instance the fort was not some distance from the village

centre. Indeed modern Ebchester sits squarely where the fort used to be. The main street of the village could not be more appropriately named than Vindomora Road, this being the village's old Roman name.

However, the forest of TV aerials on the roofs of the grey stone houses may seem a little out of character. But Ebchester is in a deep hollow of the Derwent valley, and the surrounding escarpments, beautiful as they are, make viewing sometimes a hazardous exercise. You find this a primary complaint, wherever you go in the village.

Ebchester is best approached, I suppose, via the controversial switchback and flyover bridge at Scotswood, and the road to it and the glories of the Derwent goes through a series of industrial hamlets, Axwell, Winlaton and Rowlands Gill, and against an occasional backcloth of steam and smoke. However, once past Rowlands Gill, the valley is revealed with its fields sweeping upwards and its wooded skyline. There are numerous gentle and rural pathways down to the river and upward to Medomsley and Leadgate. The valley reaches its truest beauty at Ebchester for here all signs of industry have been cast away. The road which approaches the river is (when thick with snow and ice) of a truly terrifying steepness, but the quiet which invests the whole valley is absolutely compelling. I have never seen picnic spots so delectable and so free from other humans.

The church at Ebchester is unexceptional though its name— St Ebbas—is certainly highly unusual, there being, it is said, only two other churches in the country similarly named. The village in the 1970s, though, is unconcerned with matters of ancient history but considers itself fortunate—as undoubtedly it is—to have been allowed to remain so serene and unaltered. The clock in the church tower will always stand at ten to three, one feels.

The same, broadly speaking, is true of Shotley Bridge, a mile or two further westward, a bigger village of similar grey stone, Victorian or early Edwardian, and as quiet and undisturbed on a summer Saturday or Sunday as would incur the envy of those seething villages in the South. There used to be a paper mill here, and a corn mill, and a spa where the waters were so therapeutic that they guaranteed a cure for scurvy. Most unusual though, was the German swordmaking industry and how it came to the village. On the face of things this would seem wildly improbable—but it happened. The swordmakers, refugees from religious persecution, came to England in 1685. They were skilled beyond anything known to English artisans in the tempering of steel, and they were concerned—even in exile—to preserve the secrets of their craft. Thus it became imperative to move away from the prying eyes of London and they arrived in the North, it seemed, because its great remoteness would guarantee them a reasonable security. Once here they examined the banks of the Tyne and then, when this scrutiny failed to provide an ideal situation, moved westwards from the confluence of Tyne and Derwent. At Shotley Bridge they found that the water, one of their greatest considerations, was precisely of the required softness. Additionally there were abundant supplies of excellent iron stone in the neighbouring hills, and the locality —heaven knows—was sufficiently secluded. So here they rested and prospered for more than a hundred years. The swords of Shotley were perfectly formed and "equal in finish flexibility and strength to the most distinguished blades of Damascus and Toledo", and the long swords were the most marvellous weapons of the English army.

Generation after generation prospered prodigiously, and William Oley, a descendent of one of the original emigrants, who died in 1810, was said to own most of the village of Shotley. In time, of course, production secrets became irrelevant, and with the discovery of the rifle the industry declined and eventually ceased altogether. But descendants of the original families are still in the region, and there are several Oleys in the local telephone directory to prove it.

Returning from Shotley, one of the many side roads goes to Chopwell which, by any standards, is a place of quite astonishing attainment. In all the history in Britain of industrial strife there is nowhere else, I am tolerably certain, where events so remarkable occurred and where the memory of them is still so vivid.

In the General Strike of 1926 Chopwell, because of the militancy of its miners, acquired the name of little Moscow. It was a time, of course, when the romantic view of the Russian Revolution was still widely held and in Chopwell this view was translated into action in a highly dramatic way. For instance the Union Jack flying at the council offices was pulled down and the hammer and sickle raised in its stead and—it was said though I have never been able to confirm this—that the Bible was taken from the chapel pulpit and the works of Karl Marx were substituted. Subsequent to this, streets on new council estates were named after Lenin, Engels and Marx and during the strike a militant news-sheet was produced from a clandestine HQ in the council offices. Arising from the general disturbance, the council chairman, who was a dynamic and dominating character, was arrested, as was Will Lawther, then a militant miners' leader. Will was eventually knighted as Sir William, and became known as an outstanding moderate. He spent his time in gaol reading the Bible "from cover to cover". Asked why he did so he replied that it passed the time, and anyway, there was no other reading matter. Chopwell, inviolate Labour stronghold though it continues to be, has long since given up its romantic militancy and is now something of a depressed place without *raison d'etre*—the pits having long gone. It labours also under the severest handicap of being sited almost wholly on the side of a steep hill as the road straggles at an acute angle out of the foot of the Derwent Valley.

Still, a social life, gravitating as it does round the club and the bingo hall, continues in a vivid way, and compensation for the tortuous incline is provided when one reaches a plateau near the golf course. From here the view over the Derwent is breathtaking. The Chopwell Woods, now run commercially by the Forestry Commission but still a delectable picnicking place in summer, provided the timber for the first of Britain's three-deck battleships, the *Royal Sovereign*, some time in the middle seventeenth century. They felled 2,500 oak trees for this purpose and shipped them to London via Blaydon and the Tyne.

Blaydon, another village one meets after the long journey down from the Chopwell heights, has acquired national—maybe even international—eminence simply because of the compelling nature of its folklore. It is decidedly unprepossessing, the dereliction arising from the dross of mining, tar works, coke works, not to mention junkyards and disused allotments and piggeries, presenting as dismal a picture as may well be imagined. Much resuscitation is in the air. There is already a new shopping centre and 120 acres of the worst of the blight is to be cleared away in due course, encouraging the rare plants which—unbelievably—still grow in the environs of Blaydon Burn, and the setts of badgers which are said to thrive there. The red squirrel also multiplies here, living in the shadow of the junkyards. Blaydon, like Chopwell, has its tradition of implacable radicalism. In the last century, for instance, they welcomed Garibaldi, but were not so forthcoming when Joseph Cowen, an industrialist of liberal leanings, decided that a statue should commemorate his visit to the village. Cowen raised the money by a one-penny levy on each of his employees—a decision they did not appreciate. So they toppled the statue, and local historians recently instituted a search for it after rumours that it still—after all these years—rested in some forgotten corner of the council tip. But it was not there. The belief now is that the irate workers actually threw the statue in the river—but nobody is quite sure. The real fame of Blaydon, if fame is the right word, rests on *The Blaydon Races*, the song which popular newspapers insist is the anthem of the Geordies. The song, written by George Ridley, and first sung in Balmbra's Music Hall in Newcastle in June 1862, celebrates the journey from Newcastle to Blaydon to see the races. There are six verses to this song and hardly anyone knows the words except for the first verse and the rousing chorus. It begins like this:

Aa went to Blaydon Races, 'twas on the ninth of Joon,
Eiteen hundred an' sixty two, on a summer's efternoon.
Aa tyuk the 'bus fra' Balmbra's, an' she wis heavy laden,
Away we went along Collingwood Street, that's on the road te
Blaydon.

The chorus, repeated after each verse is:

O! lads, ye shud a' seen us gannin',
Passin the foaks alang the road just as they wor stannin';
Thor wis lots o' lads an' lasses there, aall wi' smiling faces,
Gannin' alang the Scotswood Road, te see th' Blaydon Races.

This and the rest is a true account of a happening: the races were held from 1861 until 1916 when they were disbanded because of a riot. But it is only in the last decade or two that the song and what it implies has been so enthusiastically taken up. The Northumberland and Durham Tourist Association, for instance, have seized on the situation as a priceless way of publicizing the area, and the ubiquitous Geordie has become a tourist attraction. Journalists have retraced the steps of the racegoers and reached a cautious agreement as to where, in Blaydon, the races were held. But it is perhaps the adoption by the supporters of Newcastle and Sunderland football clubs of the song as their own which freely provides it with its widest circulation. When these fans travel to Liverpool, or London or Manchester or Birmingham, for example, they collect like tribalists celebrating some mystic rite, and bellow forth the chorus as each crisis in the game arises. It is used to celebrate in victory, to commiserate in defeat, as a battle cry when victory is near, and as a collective yell of defiance if the opposition is simply superior. There are undoubtedly better songs of Durham and the Tyne, more romantic, and less associated with what, in all probability, was a pretty drunken outing. Yet this is the anthem and the reason, almost solely, why the name of Blaydon is known all over the uncivilized world.

As a footnote to all this I journeyed separately to Castleside, Muggleswick and Edmundbyers. Castleside, on the periphery of Consett, still looks like a frontier village though it sits squarely on the A68. However, as you turn on to this busy main road towards Corbridge, you are on the very edge of Durham and Northumberland and there is, by any standard, a remarkable instance of this juxtaposition of town and country which continually confronts you in Durham.

Down the steep incline of the road you stop the car and looking right across two fields there is a vista of eight chimneys alternatively belching white, grey and acrid orange smoke. There are, in addition, wasp-waisted cooling towers and corrugated industrial skyscrapers all fronted by dross heaps of grey scree and a collection of dingy housing.

Looking left, however, there are endless stone walls, fields, silence, nothing. The contrast is eerie and is enhanced if the clouds are lowering, scudding across the skyline, and there is more than a hint of rain. This weather is almost normal.

A few miles on and the turn left towards Edmundbyers brings the narrow road precisely to the border of the two counties. The vast empty moorlands towards Stanhope Common and the approach to Weardale are scarcely relieved except for a glint of water which is the Derwent Reservoir which is a considerable haunt of anglers. The Derwent is a delectable place in summer and it shines like an elongated silver fish in the sunshine as you view it from a distance. On summer weekends the dead roads leap to life, the boat races attracting up to a couple of thousand spectators, but lest the multitude should forget the serious purpose of all this watery paradise, there is a reminder that, come 2001, we will all have automatic dish-washers, sprinklers in our gardens and take two baths a week, consuming water far more prodigiously than now. The boating crowds and the angling few are heedless and when October comes they depart and the Derwent returns to its solitude.

A devious offshoot takes one to Muggleswick—it is even in summer an isolated and antique land here with two houses, a farm and a telephone kiosk. The horned, blackfaced hill sheep clutter the roads, sluggish, unafraid, and so contemptuous nowadays of the motor car that they will scarce move. Rustlers raid hereabouts and in many another isolated spot and are almost impossible to stop. The technique is pathetically simple: just a fast car with a capacious boot. Once the sheep retreated in terror as cars approached, but now they are conditioned and impassive as you drive past. So it is easy to pick up a couple and, bashing them to death, load them in the boot and away. I imagine, though, that many a rustler must have been disconcerted with the meat that finally reached his table: that is if the sheep are as tough as they look.

10

Journey into Weardale

WEARDALE began for me with a fumbling sort of investigation into Saxon mystery and ended 2,000 feet up on the fells contemplating a brown, patchwork panorama. In between these—for me—unique impressions, days went by and the weather changed from April winter to April summer. At times the slanting snow and suddenly lowering clouds made me retreat hurriedly into pubs and take part in dizzying assorted conversation. At times the skies were so blue, the waters so clear and undisturbed, and the streets of the linear villages so quiet, that one could not imagine storms raging.

In a week I found the dale a mass of fascinating contradictions and contrasts so that within a minute—and this happened—I could be watching the belated and demented dance of the mad March Hare in the stubble and then leaping for life from the path of a juggernaut as it swivelled round the bend of a narrow country road. More of juggernauts in due course since they are an important if regrettable part of the contemporary life of the dale. But no more of the hare, or the disappearing wake of the otter. These were rare and cherished fragments of the country scene and not to be repeated.

One nice point in approaching Weardale has to be settled before any journey of exploration can really begin. Do you start in the heights beyond Wearhead, cascading downwards as the valley gets wider and softer to Witton-le-Wear and beyond? It is the fashionable way of most pilgrims both past and present. For if you view the problem historically so much activity was concentrated in the area where the Wear approaches its source. Today the tourist from the more formidable delights of Teesdale also arrives at points near the head of the Wear. So does the foray from the north, either from Alston, which is in Cumberland, or Allenheads which, though it has much in common, both historically and contemporaneously with the Weardale villages, is, in fact in Northumberland.

For myself, though I have sped up and down the dale, I like best the gradual intrusion from Bishop Auckland, and though there are certain Wagnerian echoes in heavy weather which those of appropriately gloomy temperament find satisfying, the journey is best accomplished when the sun shines, the moorland grasses grow quickly, and the foliage is thick on the trees. When these—admittedly rare—conditions persist for a few days, even the occasional industrial excrescence is enlivened, and the breathless struggles to the heights of Kilhope or Burtree or Welhope at journey's end is rewarded with a view which is full value for the massive energy expended. But this is always a gamble for at 2,000 feet or so, views dissolve quickly into nothing except thin curls of mist and the sudden vague shapes of the tough, mountain sheep.

Best of all, of course, is to see the dale in all its guises and at every season, for the ski-ing at Swinhope Moor above Westgate is a fine sight, as is the ice glistening on the reservoirs at Burnhope or Tunstall. You do not see that often.

Whatever you do, however you approach this most unassuming of dales, a certain elucidation is at first imperative. There are facts and figures one has to know. There is, for instance, an area of 100,000 acres, and a sparse population of only 8,000 which, however, shows little sign of growing less. It is a dale which, by common consent, does not approach the grandeur of the Tees, especially in its upper reaches. But with its deep valleys and hills rising precipitously it is really more like Tynedale, though of course, its history and social development have been very different. It is a place of lovely, sweet-sounding names: Heathering Dell, Hanging Wells, Bintree Linn, Harehope Ghyll, Daddryshields and many more. Pre-eminently, perhaps, as a glance at a contour map quickly shows, it is a land of close, high hills, brown in the dusk and burnished in the summer sun. The head of the dale rests on Burnhope Seat, Malaksoff and Kilhope Law, and drops from 1,104 feet at Wearhead to 500 feet at Wolsingham. From any vantage point of 2,000 feet or over the view is said (for I did not count them) to take in sixteen hills of this approximate height.

From the air at perhaps 10,000 feet the rushing experience is prodigious. The scars caused by glacial action are clearly visible; the hills look like serried ranks of small protuberances, and the uprush of air causes light aircraft to be flung exhilaratingly about the sky. The pilot of an executive jet from Newcastle Airport who imparted this free information added the warning: "If you are prone to air sickness, seek another route."

The Wear itself is formed by three streams: first the Kilhope Burn which is joined at Lanehead by the Welhope Burn. These waters merge at Wearhead with Burnhope Burn at the Win Pool, and thereafter the flow eastwards is known as the Wear. Constantly it is swelled by burns at Ireshope, Harthope, Daddry, Swinhope, Westernhope and Horsley from the south, and Middleshope Yellock, Rookhope and Stanhope Burns to the north. There are other becks, rivulets, cascades and waterfalls. It is, for some miles, a gorgeous meandering river, but sadly merges too quickly into the Durham coalfield and then becomes polluted and ordinary. The dale, I suppose, could end anywhere, even at Sunderland where the wide Wear meets the sea. More properly, though, it could be said to have expended itself at Bishop Auckland. This was my assumption, and was also excessively convenient since I proposed exploration, first of all, of the hidden hamlet of Escomb. This has aspects which are not only unique in the world, but the village itself is infernally difficult to find.

In search, therefore, of Saxon splendour, and a church that is a thrilling and totally composed relic of the distant past, I reached Bishop Auckland, assuming that a place of such world importance in the neighbourhood would be well signposted, the directions, maybe, emblazoned for all to see. Not so. Escomb skilfully hides the fact that it is just around the corner. But I persevered and in due course and after considerable mischance discovered a signpost to High Etherley. A policeman assured me that somewhere along the road, at a tiny T-junction was the simple sign: Escomb, Saxon Church. There it was on the left a couple of miles on and I turned, drove quickly and now excitedly, and speedily became lost in the wilds of Toft Hill.

A fundamental error as it turned out. I retraced to the junction, turned right, and soon enough was in the very heart of Escomb. This is a remote colliery hamlet, the pit long gone. Even the pit heap has been grassed; the colliery houses have been replaced by spruce council semis. And there, opposite a newish-looking pub called 'The Saxon' (which turns out to be a little expensive for the locals) and also facing a Saxon village green, is the most precious and mysterious of churches in the North.

I have no feeling for the detail of church architecture and have explicitly avoided the churches in the villages in this book unless there is a compelling human reason to do otherwise. Escomb, though, is the marvellous exception to this rule. The other churches in the North-east that are as old are St Paul's at Jarrow, St Peter's at Monkwearmouth and St Andrew's at Corbridge. All have their known history and have been adorned and added to throughout the generations. They have been subject to endless celebrations and scrutiny from archaeologists. Stop a child in the streets of Jarrow or Sunderland and they will tell you (I daresay) of the close local identification with St Bede, and of the churches of his era in the neighbourhood that now are the subject of much communal pride.

But nothing is known of the church at Escomb, nor, apart from a twelfth-century porch has the structure been changed. The Victorians, those unknowing desecrators of ancient things, patently did not know that Escomb existed. So now, in 1975, the unassuming little church stands just as the Saxons built it in this unlikely place, and no one knows why or how. A nineteenth-century Bishop of Durham observed: "I think that it is distinctive of Escomb that it has no history. It is just a little obscure church, probably preserved by its lack of importance, which has managed to survive."

And there it is, locked, but the key is hanging on the door of a cottage nearby which, in this age of vandals, shows a trusting nature. The stones of this simple structure, smoothed and hollowed with time look incredibly old, and there is no doubt that in a sense they are second hand. In about 675 they were seemingly lugged across from the disused and ruined Roman station at Binchester a couple of miles away. Higher up on the walls the stones are rougher and smaller; these are new—simple Saxon stones used when the Roman supply had become exhausted. Inside the church is tiny; tall and dignified, but miniscule. What fascinates your imagination is how it was before it was discovered in 1875. For until then, until Dr Hooppell, the Vicar of Byers Green not far away, pronounced on its great antiquity, it seems to have been totally ignored. Indeed a new parish church had been built on the top of the hill in 1863, the Saxon church being relegated to the status of a chapel, and seemingly in dire need of repair. Bishop Lightfoot launched a public appeal for funds, and the repairs were carried out. But the church still languished as a dusty, scarcely used, neglected ecclesiastical museum until, during the incumbency of Mr Lee who was vicar of Escomb from 1959 to 1964, it was decided to restore and refurnish the old church. It was given a heating and lighting system; new altar, seating and other furniture, without in any way attempting to recreate a Saxon interior.

High Force, an impressive spectacle

Middleton in Teesdale, surrounded by Durham and Yorkshire

Frosterley, where marble is still quarried

Wolsingham, where there is a steelworks

Gainford: old and new

This water should
be boiled before
using for
drinking purposes

Great Stainton. (*Above*) The water pump commemorating Queen
Victoria's Jubilee

Middleton-One-Row on the Tees

The extensive green at Hurworth

The conical stone on the green at Sadberge. It is a relic of the Ice Age

Raby Castle, centre of the Rising of the North

Now it is the parish church again, the edifice at the top of the hill having been pulled down. Perhaps, on reflection, it is better for being lost in a hamlet on the Wear rather than being marketed in the intense fashion of some ancient buildings. And as for the signpost which unfailingly guides people the wrong way—perhaps that is better left as it is.

From Escomb one arrives soon enough at Fir Tree which lingers at the entrance to Weardale without in any way being part of it. Fir Tree—the coniferous wood on its outskirts explaining the name —is a hamlet, the distinction of which seems to lie entirely with 'The Duke of York', an old pub refurbished, which denies every spit and sawdust criticism I make about Durham village pubs in general in another chapter.

'The Duke' is comfortable, welcoming (the snowstorm, of course, having driven me inside), has a decent sandwich on a decent plate, no juke-box, crisps, nuts or fruit machine, and a small restaurant of unadventurous pub food meticulously and quickly served. There are guns and antique sporting prints on the white walls, and on the counter a magnificent Victorian bottle opener, complicated and, of course, a sure conversation point. Wind the wheel and out pops the cork. But—and this may be the ultimate test of a good pub—the conversation even among strangers, fizzes round the room. There is a hilarious discussion about inbreeding in nine-teenth-century Weardale. An attack is made on middle-class in-tellectuals, liberals (why liberals?) and people with beards. Another attack on environmentalist protests at the sinking of new fluospar mines in the dales. No indigenous countryman is against these mines (we will be writing a lot more about fluospar including ex-plaining what it is) because they bring more employment and keep the young people in the dale. Then poetry. The magistrate, fresh from a preliminary hearing of a messy case of rape recalls another case years ago in a town not far away, where the defendant ex-plained his guilt by quoting Gerard Manley Hopkins: "It wasn't I who sinned the sin; My ruthless body dragged me in." He got seven years. Hearing that I have been to Escomb, the magistrate asks if I saw the Kipling poem on the wall. I say I missed it, whereupon he quotes it in its entirety. It is about a Christian priest who could not get people to go to his service because the heathen Saxons were roistering and ended up preaching the word to a bullock and a donkey. Somehow it conveys the atmosphere at Escomb more efficiently than 10,000 words of prose. He recites the first two stanzas again so I can copy them down:

H

Eddi, Priest of St Wilfred, at the Chapel of Manhood End;
Ordered a midnight service for such as cared to attend.
But the Saxons were keeping Christmas and the night was stormy,
  as well,
Nobody came to the service, though Eddi rang the bell.

The magistrate, before departing, says he is good at remembering items of disconnected information and must really take part in a TV quiz game one of these days. I leave too, the snow having ceased and the sun is palely loitering out of heavy clouds. And so to the roundabout at Harperley and on to the A689 which is the real road through the dale.

This is the road of the juggernauts. In the days of the boom in lead mining early in the nineteenth century it was a dusty track and even now, west of Stanhope, it narrows to old country standards. There is a big limestone-quarrying business—unlike the lead mining, this has survived—and this especially applies to the south of Stanhope on the Barnard Castle road where there is an eerie lunar landscape. There is another big development at Heights Quarry not far away, and both these and other enterprises involve many small hauliers with massive lorries, many of which serve the steel works at Consett. It was against the menace of one of these that I leapt for life, just after watching the mad April hare.

Limestone quarrying, though, is an easy life now, relatively speaking. It seems to have begun, at any rate in a biggish way about 150 years ago at Stanhope and there were also large quarries operating at Frosterley. It seems that half a dozen large quarries which had a combined output of about 1,000 tons a day were the making of these two villages. There are plenty of the older people particularly in Stanhope today who will give you stories of the grindingly hard life their forbears lived. How they worked in those days!

For there they were, exposed to all the weather and before the age of machinery, using heavy, noisy tools. There was a particularly vicious flat hammer, weighing about sixteen pounds which they wielded to break the stone. Sometimes as many as a hundred trucks were being filled simultaneously at a big Stanhope quarry, and the trucks took up to a dozen tons. The men were paid about a shilling a ton which arbitrarily was reduced to sixpence if times were hard. The bigger the stones you flung in the trucks, the greater the physical stress upon yourself, but the quicker you made your pitiful wage. But it was far more profitable for the owners if the stones were smaller and they had inspectors patrolling the ranges above the quarries, rather like prison guards at the old Alcatraz, seeing that this situation was achieved. Being a limestone worker, therefore, in the middle of the Industrial Revolution was really a terrible life. Men became old before their time; they succumbed to what nowadays would be recognized as heart disease, hernias from the strain of that flat hammer, rheumatism, accidents of every sort, and all the dust ailments to which the early coalminer was prone. The limestone quarrier often enough died young as did his lead-mining colleague. Anywhere in the dale, in the churchyards of Stanhope, Wolsingham, Frosterley and Wearhead, not to mention Tow Law which is not really part of Weardale at all, you will see the evidence: gravestones with the epitaphs of miners and quarriers who died in their late thirties and early forties. They had stout Biblical names: Ezekial, Zacharia, Matthew, Luke, John. They were fathers of large families, and they died young because the limestone and the lead had entered their souls. Their lives, as someone said in another connection, were nasty, brutish and short, though often enough spurred on by the hope of the hereafter given them by the Methodist religion which gripped the dale so strongly.

The real industrial romance of the dale, though, is enshrined in the story of lead. White lead was mined in the days of King Stephen, and long before deep mining came they scavenged the surface of the dale in the search for the mineral. Hundreds of acres were torn, and enormous quantities of the debris were washed from the hillsides into the streams. The evidence is there to this day with the stone heaps and gullies and the curious corrugated look some hillsides have. In the early part of the nineteenth century at least thirty-four lead mines were being worked in the dale: twenty to the north side and fourteen to the south, and this was the time when the Beaumont family, later to be ennobled as the Allendales, held the lease of many of the mines. This was the time, also, of high prosperity for the owners, and a drama, at least in retrospect, about the lead miners' task that thrills the imagination, aware as we must be of how slavish were their lives. Everybody worked in mining: in 1821 thirty-six mines were in full swing in the dales. The technique was to drive levels and drifts into the hillsides near essential water for the washing of the lead from the limestone.

Then, simply, they followed the vein of lead wherever it went. Great depths and heights were reached with a succession of ladders, but it was an erratic, not to say imponderable task. Often enough the veins would disappear and men would labour for weeks without reward. For this reason subsistence wages of ten shillings a week were introduced, and then balances were struck each half year. These were the times of great rejoicing for if rich veins had been struck payouts could be as much as £100. Weddings were arranged for these times; the fairs came to places like Stanhope and set up in the main street. The silver bands for which Weardale was famous held their contests, and on one occasion so great was the demand—to hear the finest of them—it was improbably named Bessie's o' the Barn—that there was not a place in St John's Chapel big enough to house all the people. So they held it in the open—approximately 150 years before the first open-air pop concert. Bare-fist fighting, engaged in often enough after drinking contests, took place in hastly improvized moorland arenas. One fanciful gentleman wrote that you could hear the sounds of the blows a mile away. There was step dancing, and much of the famous Cumberland-style wrestling, Cumberland being just over the fells. All the itinerants of the time seemed to be attracted to the merry-making; tramps by the score, pedlars, Scotch drapers, scissor grinders, German bands, wandering preachers, then, of course, it was back to slavery. Unlike the coalminers, some of the men had to travel considerable distances to their work and they went by donkey. At the mine accommodation was in shops or lodges and the man stayed a week at a time. They carried their belongings in wallets, cooked their own food, and slept, twenty or more to a room in contrivances like ships' bunks. Conditions were squalid.

You first went down the lead mine at the age of eight; fathers used to carry the small boys down the ladders to depths of up to sixty fathoms—until they could cope with the perilous ladders themselves. The villages and hamlets reverberated to the sound of heavy clogs as the boys went to work at five o'clock in the morning.

They were grotesquely clad—you could buy and it was expedient to do so, the discarded red coat of a soldier for a shilling. They did work for twelve hours a day—work that was far too heavy for them like shovelling lead ore and waste, for eight-pence. If the lad survived he graduated to become a proper miner, often enough to join a partnership which would include his father.

These partnerships included from four to twelve men. Each would wear heavy clogs with thick iron round the soles and carry home-made lanterns. Fatal accidents (unlike the holocaust of the early coal mining) were rare, though there were examples of men being crushed by falling stones, and some instances of entombment. Within the folklore of the early lead mining are tales of trapped men eating tallow candles to keep alive, and getting water as it dripped thinly down the side of the rise.

The lead used to be carried away from the mines by galloways, hardy little horses about a dozen hands high, each of which carried two hundredweights of lead on its saddle. These horses were without bridles, but muzzled to avoid the grazing of lead-contaminated grass. They moved away from the mines in strings of twenty-five or so, and the leader would have a bell attached to his neck. As they went through the hamlets on the terrible roads: thick with dust in summer and mud or snow and ice in winter, people came to the cottage doors to see the quiet spectacle. The galloways lasted until 1875, and then, with the better roads they were succeeded by yuhr (ore) carts which would take the lead to Allenheads and bring back timber for the mines.

The industry, though, was never again to reach the zenith it achieved in the early nineteenth century. The veins ran out. And where they did not, the importation of cheap Spanish ore from the 1860s onwards closed many mines and drove the miners to the burgeoning coal industry in north-west Durham. The sad momentum of closure quickened to such a degree that the population of the dale diminished by 2,000 from 1871 to 1891.

It was never to be revived, though areas of lead-mining activity persisted and as late as 1910 the Weardale Lead Co. got 3,700 tons from its five mines.

Coinciding with all this was the mining for iron and the processing of the ore. They got the ore out of the ground at many places in Upper Weardale, both by deep mining and open cast. The first forge had been at Bedburn in 1408 and it had been fired by oak, but the great days were a hundred years ago. They made cannon balls for the Crimea at Tow Law, for example, and at their peak the furnaces at Tow Law and the mines in the upper dale employed up to 1,700 people. There were 70,000 tons mined in 1881. Again, like the workers in lead, the iron workers had a fiercely hard life. The ore was conveyed by horse and cart to the depot at Westgate with the roads ridged and slimy or deep in snow in winter, or—what was almost worse—a summer mix of dried mud and iron filings. Carts came to grief; horses fell and broke their legs on the fiendish hump-back bridge at Daddryshield, and the iron men, like their brothers in lead, often died young.

If they survived they were afflicted with crippling rheumatics and with an incurable habit of reminiscence. Simply they were proud of their hardship which they thought of as in no way exceptional.

It is all gone, of course, now, the only mining of any consequence being of a substance the Victorians cast away as waste. This is the previously referred to fluospar. It is a quartz-like product, a derivative of the lead veins, for which there seemed to be no conceivable use. Now, used both by the steel and chemical industries, it is in huge demand, since it is only to be found in Weardale and Derbyshire. There are fluospar mines all over Weardale—specifically at Rookhope, Cambo Keels and Eastgate, and there are the applications for more mines which rouse the ire of the conservationists. There is an eternal war between them and the natives and not, so far as I would judge, much personal liking either. Anyway, so entrancing is the prospect of gathering in the fluospar that licences are granted nowadays to people who scavenge the old lead spoilheaps and pick up the fluospar which has been lying there for decades. It comes in all sorts of gorgeous colours, and there is a thriving business in burnishing little bits of the stuff for costume jewellery and rings.

Back, though, after so much diversion to that roundabout at Harperley, where the impression of an actual doorway opening to the dale is an acute one. It is, as it were, a turn into an ancient land; not only does the topography suggest this—the immediately brooding hills after the brisk flat lands of the A68. In addition to this there is the intense feeling of timelessness, so that it dawns on you in a forcible way that this is how it was long before the dramas of the lead and iron mines, and before the coming of the Methodists who knelt in the snow of the hills to make their conversion.

Wesley may greet the dalesmen as "beautiful" people, and the impact of the Primitive Methodists may be so great that the cynical would say that all the people were turning into ranters. All this happened, but the tumult of the early nineteenth century, the dale compellingly suggests, was really just a moment ago.

It is an impression which is reinforced with more intimate knowledge of the hill lands, where the drystone walling stretches endlessly away, and the the farms cling to the sides as far up as 1,200 feet. There is a veritable maze of pathways across the fells, some of them going back to the Bronze Age. Others were used by Scottish drovers who avoided the valley because of the fear of ambush. There are a lot of caves, too, in the limestone sides of the dale at places like Ireshope, Ludwell and Westernhope, and it is easy enough, faced with all this evidence of great antiquity, to let your mind range back. The dale used to be thickly forested with all the game for which medieval England was famous. Nowadays fox, badger, stoat, weasel, grouse, rabbit, hare, and owl remain, as the rare otter does too.

One of those caves did provide evidence of the distant past, and it is all the more fascinating because, it seems, the evidence is in isolation. In 1850 workmen digging at the Linkirk Caves, near Stanhope, discovered a collection of bronze and golden implements indubitably the property of a rich family from the late Bronze Age. These included a gold armlet, an amber necklace, a bronze razor and buckets, several bronze spearheads and fragments of pottery. The bucket was one of the signs of prestige of that age, and there was also found a cheek-piece and bits with part of a wheel—all of which seemed to indicate that horses were worked in those days. One mystery, though, which no one completely could elucidate, was why all this evidence of richness was found where it was. There were also three skulls, indicating, perhaps that a whole family had been here. But why? No wealthy Bronze Age man would live in a cave. Perhaps, it has been suggested, they were hiding from their enemies and, asleep in the cave, were drowned by a rapidly rising mountain stream. The find was said to give the first definite indication both of the domestication of the horse and the use of wheeled vehicles in the British Isles.

Weardale nowadays, though, concerns itself with more immediate matters. Although there is no sign of depopulation, nor any reduction, village by village, in the number of people, the fears of decisive change are always present. The fear is not that the dales population will grow less, because there is a long queue for the limited number of weekend cottages which are taken mostly by the prosperous from Tyneside and Wearside, and the number of caravanners increases every year. Feelings about the caravans are decidedly mixed, there now being 1,500 in the dale. Some of them are subtly sited, other simply spoil the area, the example being the seventy in the centre of Stanhope, and another site at Witton Castle widely described to me as uninspired, unimaginative and, at times, decidedly tatty. These are sentiments which invite a large measure of agreement.

The substantial fear of the natives is that job opportunities for young people will become so limited that more and more will be forced away to industrial Wearside. This is the principal reason why you will seldom find a dalesman joining the protestors at the sinking of new fluospar mines. Neither do they agree with that knowledgeable man of Weardale, J. E. Morris, who complained of the "terrible disfigurement" which was "cruelly imposed on the village" of Wolsingham by the steelworks. It is certainly disconcerting suddenly to descend upon the steelworks at the eastern end of the village, but they employ 400, are constantly prosperous, and can even be defended historically, since they are part of the fabric of the dale. The same could be said of the cement works at Eastgate a little further westward. These even more dramatically seem to be imposed on the fell side, for here there is no urban introduction to them as at Wolsingham. The works belch steam and the dust gives adjacent trees the resemblance of a petrified forest. Pipeworks thread their way up the hill to another factory right at the fell top from which smoke or steam continuously pour. The fells would look better without the cement making— but 400 more people are employed here. Take the romantic view and you deplore the sudden excrescence: be realistic and you take the view that the works at Wolsingham and Eastgate are the lifeblood of the dales.

Many of these villages suffer from a lack of pubs of real character; they have been described to me as "good of the sawdust variety" and I do not think that is uncharitable. A couple of good ones at Wolsingham, though, are said to be 'The Black Bull' and 'The Bay Horse', and nearby at St John's Chapel there are four pubs for a population of only 800 plus, of course, the rush of townsmen in cars and caravans in the summer. Between St John's—it got its name from an old chapel of ease—and Irehopeburn there is Ken Rowney's *hacienda*-type country club which caters for riding and fishing, and the food is said to be good. At Stanhope they complain of a good hotel which became an old peoples home as a "tragic loss of amenity", and another complaint of this straggling but pleasant capital of the dale is the use to which Stanhope Castle is now put.

Nobody pretends that the castle is in any way remarkable. Morris dismisses it as that "too conspicuous sham" which was built in 1798. Nowadays, though, it is in use, as an approved school, and I report that the locals feel resentful at the amenities which seem to be heaped on the boys, especially in sport, whereas within the village there is scarcely a decent football pitch.

At Frosterley there is a singularly beautiful church, a speck of a village green, too great an incidence of those juggernauts previously referred to, while the locals confess also to being perplexed by the summer traffic from Wearside to the Lake District. The village is also the home, of course, of the renowned Frosterley marble, which is still quarried, and was said to provide as much ornamentation for buildings in the North as Purbeck marble does in the South. It was much used in medieval times for fonts, recumbent effigies, altar slabs, grave covers and the like, and is not a conventional marble at all. Rather it is no more than a crystallized limestone which is crowded with the bones of fishes. You can see it in its natural state in the rocks at the Bollihope burn, and also at White Kerkley, a hamlet near Frosterley.

I have mentioned the ski-ing at Swinhope Moor, near Westgate, a village, incidentally, once a noted cock-fighting centre. Some of the *aficianados* of this bloody art also congregated at Daddryshield, a hamlet which, without some alertness, one may nowadays miss altogether. The Daddryshield birds, though, were of a noted fierceness and lasting power. I enquired about this and was told by an old man whose grandfather bred famous birds, that you had to have a ruthless streak to encourage the cock's innate savagery, and get it to just the right pitch of ravenous ill-temper before a match. The ruthlessness nowadays seems to have departed entirely, and Daddryshield is a useful and welcoming place for walkers.

The rest, as they say, is silence, the quietude at Wearhead and Cowshill being in every respect remarkable. Wearhead, where the river (and therefore really the dale) begins is cosy, usually brisk (it is at over 1,100 feet) and utterly dominated by the Burnhope Reservoir on its outskirts. It is from here, though, or perhaps from Cowshill, that I recommend an expedition of the kind briefly referred to at the beginning of this chapter. This is to take a clear day, journey a little further north and west on the Alston road, striking across country to high land on the Welhope Moor. Here (or at a dozen other vantage points) to look down on the not inconsiderable glories of the dale I have tried to convey. Memorable indeed.

But though I traversed the dale the wrong way, and became diverted in so many ways, I kept to myself, like a child hoarding the last strawberry on its plate, a final small expedition from Wolsingham back eastward on the south side of the river. I did this because of a conviction born of a similar journey some years ago, that this was the most delectable fragment of all of Weardale. I was deterred for several weeks from completing the Weardale exploration, and this was an exceedingly fortunate circumstance since when I did so, winter was gone at last, the trees were in full leaf, and the eastward journey lived up to its most fascinating reputation.

Once across the river at Wolsingham on the south side, and industry is banished. The Wear is wide at this point but shallow and rocky with deep isolated pools. Fishermen in long waders are casting in the middle of the river as I pass, but the whole scene is spoiled by the ubiquitous caravan site, small but glaringly obvious. Local opinion here and subsequently at the end of the Weardale journey at Witton-le-Wear is massively indifferent towards the caravanners, reckoning that it is a nonsense to suggest that they contribute much to the local economy. The caravanners bring their groceries from the towns since supermarket prices are cheaper than those in the village shops. Do they then patronize the pubs? It is difficult to see how the four pubs in St John's Chapel could endure without them. Yet at Witton-le-Wear the landlady at 'The Victoria' insisted that she was not concerned for their patronage and that they liked the town life of Crook a couple of miles away.

From the river at Wolsingham the road winds steeply upwards, and the judgement of Morris who calls this one of the most beautiful journeys in the whole of Durham is amply confirmed.

The rolling fields are parcelled into neat plots by endless miles of drystone walls; there is scarcely a dividing hedge in sight. I have seen nowhere in the country where the walls are so precise, so geometrical and tidy. Looking north from the heights above Wolsingham they stretch high and to the far horizon, spreading, proliferating. The stones are in the same pattern as those used in the church at Escomb, uneven chunks of sandstone and limestone. You wonder at the sheer accomplishment. In the sixteenth and seventeenth centuries when the moors and the heights were thus divided the creation of the walling must have been a massive operation the like of which we can scarcely conceive of today. The moors must have been covered by hundreds of experts; otherwise the job would never have been done.

Yet now drystone walling is a dying art. I have seen it demonstrated in ideal conditions at agricultural shows, but you search almost in vain for a professional exponent in the dale today —and surely they must need one.

They do indeed, for the walls, so durable, are beginning to collapse. A few hundred years of moorland storms and of cows and sheep pushing at them are bringing the walls tumbling down— not to any dramatic extent, of course, but in sufficient momentum to bring greater demand for his services than the only drystone waller in the territory can ever fulfil.

I found John Bell in a bleak, isolated farmyard 1,000 feet up on the moors just above Satley. He was basically a dairy farmer and he came from the softer lands around Durham City where his father's farm had its fields decently divided by hedges. John embraced the tough life of hill farming on forty-six acres above Satley twelve years ago and discovered two things—that walls stretched in every direction, and that there was a pronounced degree of dilapidation about some of them. He discovered also that, since the stone lay just beneath the few inches of poor hill soil, there were small hill quarries everywhere from which—in the years past —the stone had been dug.

He became a drystone waller by the simple method of trial and error, spurred on by economic necessity when he found dairy farming such a parlous way of making a living. So he abandoned milk producing; took on a few cows for breeding and additionally became the drystone waller to Weardale. Now he has a year's work in hand, and though he has an assistant who is learning the business he is refusing jobs every day. It is not a difficult job, he says, and you can do about five yards a day, and this will mean a wall about four and a half feet high, about two and a half feet wide at the bottom tapering to about half that at the top. The stones can vary from nearly a yard long to just a few inches, and the real skill is in having a good eye—in recognizing how a stone wall will fit with a minimum of 'dressing' with your hammer. The professional dresses and fits the stone in a minute; the well-meaning amateur (John shudders a little) is continually picking up stones and discarding them—John can lay a whole line while he is pondering on a single one.

It is a hard, solitary life, and you cannot follow your calling at 1,500 feet when the winter blizzards sweep past you, or in the extreme cold. So, it is a spring, summer and autumn job, the great satisfaction coming from the quick symmetry of your creation, and from the strength that can withstand the leaning cattle and the pushing sheep.

At Bedburn, where a rushing torrent of a rivulet comes from the south-west, there is a tiny hamlet in deep seclusion, with just a few houses, a ruined water mill, and an entrancing meadow which leads into a secluded dell. Here I found masses of primroses and— a little later—violets and bluebells. Disregard the occasional car and there is not a vestige of modernity here. I tried an experiment of sitting for an hour on a hillock above the meadow with the stream rushing by to the right, and overlooking the road. The day was a holiday, unseasonably warm and sunny, and elsewhere, even as near as Wolsingham, the cars cluttered the roads, the cafes were crowded, and noise imposed itself upon you inexorably.

Yet at Bedburn there was not a soul but myself. It is like nowhere else; not part of the Weardale personality; an isolated, blessed and odd land.

At Hamsterley which is a mile further east, the village is long, straggling, with a working men's club just turning out. The great puzzle in Hamsterley is the site of the church – or why it and the village are so set apart. The church, thirteenth century, stands in absolute isolation nearly half a mile from the village centre, and one cannot imagine old ladies, who comprise a majority congregation in so many village churches, struggling along the road on bitter, wind-swept winter evenings.

But they do, which is test enough of the toughness and resilience traditional in Weardale and of which there are many remarkable examples.

Witton-le-Wear which one reaches eventually (the road to it brings back memory of the immortal Chesterton couplet about the rolling English drunkard making the rolling English road) abounds in vigorous old ladies. They scurry everywhere in the village, sweeping pathways with zest, changing flowers in the church, talking animatedly in shop doorways, chiding dogs, chasing cats, frowning in the general direction of the caravan site and lido, walking composedly on pathways, peeping from windows, and giving the dynamic impression that hunger for life is no way diminished. I speak to the *grande dame* of all the *dames* of Witton-le-Wear who is ninety-four and young with it. She attributes her longevity (and how many boring creatures have asked her the same crass question) to hard work, good plain food, an unworried disposition and "walking everywhere". With a look of cheerful contempt at my parked car, she gives as her opinion that this last attribute is the most important of all. She also said her good health was due to the salubrity of the air. In this she has history on her side, not only in her antique use of language (when did I hear the word salubrity before?) but in the sentiment expressed. For checking on the general antecedents of the people of Witton I discovered that living a long time was not something that has just begun to occur.

The *Newcastle Chronicle* for 4th April 1778, records astonishingly that the parish register indicates no more than four funerals between March 1777 and March 1778. Of these the combined ages were 225 years—a strong testimony, the *Chronicle* avers, to "the salubrity of the air". This, I discover, was the source of the old lady's phrase. During the same period the number of children christened was nineteen. Local people, with whom I discussed these facts of history and equated them with the exhilaration of the veterans of the present, unemotionally agreed that it had always been like this. Whether, in a statistical sense, there is anything remarkable in the length of people's lives at Witton-le-Wear is unknown; what is certain is that the villagers believe this to be the case and that the evidence of zestful old age is nowhere more compelling.

As against all this there are nineteenth-century records of an overcrowded churchyard, and an attempt (unsuccessful as it turned out) by a curate named Brown to impose a surcharge for burial therein. Also in the nineteenth century, but before the aforesaid event, the Elizabethan Communion Cup was stolen from the sexton, Robert Littlefair, who kept it and other church plate under his bed. The cup departed with the lodger and was never seen again.

Dobson describes the castle at Witton-le-Wear as one of the triumphs of the Bishopric, and reckons that in its lovely groupings it excels not only Raby, which he regards as its natural rival, but also Brancepeth and Lumley both of which are not far away. He was writing about 1950 when the castle was still inhabited by the Chaytors who had been the owners from the end of the eighteenth century. Sadly the situation is much changed now, the castle being owned by Lord Lambton, the caravans securely in the castle grounds, the administrator in the castle, and the lido for campers in the parkland beside the river.

There is the old conflict here between conservative villagers and outsiders; the gap is wide and is unlikely to be bridged.

This change apart, Witton-le-Wear is brisk, friendly and unscarred by progress. The great relief for the townsman is that nothing is being built; no roads are being constructed, no roundabouts despoiling main streets. The only additions in recent years have been a few private houses built very much in character with their surroundings and twenty-five council houses carefully sited in a secluded area by the church.

There is no industry here now though there was a colliery (owned by the Chaytors), and also a company that worked a valuable seam of fire clay for sixty years.

Altogether Witton-le-Wear remains an enviable place to live

and to visit. It is also only two miles from Escomb at which forgotten hamlet you will recall my Weardale journey was begun.
Actually several weeks intervened between visiting one delectable
place and then the other. But to see them both on a single day
which I earnestly recommend, is almost a surfeit of riches, an
assault on the mind and the senses that makes this one of the
most delightful of all the journeys in Durham.

II

The Finest Dale

THE one wholly unexpected benefit conferred recently on the County of Durham has been the gift of some of the finest acres in the North Riding of Yorkshire. In the past travellers in Teesdale have observed frequently enough that the best scenery and prettiest villages were on the south bank of the river. More than once, Morris, that knowledgeable traveller, deplored that since his pilgrimage was in Durham he was prevented from straying where his fancy would otherwise have led him—that is to the south side where the gorge through which the river flowed was frequently more spectacular, the hills more violently precipitous, the villages more stately and serene.

Nowadays, and thanks to the regretted reorganization of local government which took effect from May 1974, the traveller through Durham need be inhibited in no such fashion. From the outset I decided that a fair principle was to ignore the changed boundaries so arbitrarily imposed by the planners, and to regard the county as it was before the fateful date just mentioned. Thus with the Tyne as the rough dividing line between Northumberland and Durham, the county spread conveniently and enticingly southward until the Tees was reached. This mode of operation worked well enough until planning the journey through Teesdale in some detail when I uncovered the saga of the discontented Yorkshiremen. In Teesdale bureaucracy has donated 100,000 acres of the North Riding into the reconstituted Durham, and logic dictated that these should be ignored (as being forever Yorkshire). Yet my knowledge of aggressive Yorkshire pride (and the curiosity this knowledge provoked) indicated that at least I might discover how the reluctant exiles were contemplating their fate.

To do this was a matter of relative simplicity. I was in Barnard Castle, the capital and administrative centre of the dale and intended journeying from there to Middleton in Teesdale and beyond to begin my first and formal journey down the dale. There was nothing easier, therefore, than to take the loop road on the south side of the river and reach Middleton through Lardington, Cotherstone and Romaldskirk—all of them Yorkshire to the core, but Durham, depressingly, by edict.

Well, it is true what they say. The people of these villages and, I dare say, everywhere else so mischievously annexed, are bitter at their plight. That is, when they think of such remote matters, which is seldom. They have the Englishman's natural resentment at being manipulated without consent being given, coupled with the fervent belief in the superiority of all things Yorkshire. I was not at all inclined to contest this belief especially after a confrontation with the landlord of 'The Rose and Crown' at Romaldskirk where, with the pleasant accompaniment of ham sandwiches, tomato soup and very strong beer, the subject of county boundaries naturally arose. He was a very keen supporter of Yorkshire cricket, an eloquent defender of the ways of Geoffrey Boycott, as well as the dour merits of Close and Illingworth, and he dazzled me for an hour with a paean also in praise of Emmott Robinson, Leyland, Oldroyd and similar rough-hewn characters of his youth. He then put forward a truly portentous proposition. Supposing, he argued, a son of Romaldskirk, as yet unborn, was to become, in due time, a great genius of the art of cricket: would he not, then, be disqualified from playing for Yorkshire since technically he supposed, and because of the vain idiocies of the planners, he had now been born in Durham. I made soothing noises, said I was sure the Yorkshire committee would make allowances—but he was not really assured. I left him mourning an eventuality which will probably never arise: a Yorkshireman slighted by anonymous gentlemen who never gave his problem a thought.

Barnard Castle where I began this most southern part of my pilgrimage does not really qualify for our attention since it is a market town. It is, in fact, the service and administrative area for every village in Teesdale, and is favourably placed for this role, being at the hub of a wheel from which this administration may be said to radiate. This is a considerable and diverse task since Teesdale comprises one third of the total acreage of Durham County, but has only 27,000 people. Organization from the centre in fundamental matters can become crucial for people in isolated places. It is said that Barnard Castle exudes efficiency, for example, in maintaining good roads, and in clearing the snow with a speed so that only once in fifteen years has the area largely come to a standstill. This was in 1961 when a freak storm resulted in struggling pedestrians inadvertently walking over the tops of motor cars on the road between Barnard Castle and Staindrop. Rural Teesdale converges on Barnard Castle for employment at the Glaxo factory. Work of this nature is more necessary than ever since social and economic changes in the dale have brought about a decline in quarrying, and there are far fewer farms which are also far less labour intensive. Some employment comes from random civil engineering work—three major reservoirs have been built since the war—from a glove factory at Barnard Castle and a small engineering works which gained fame and revenue in the past by the manufacture of a horse-drawn road sweeping brush which was exported all over the world.

I chanced on Barnard Castle on a day the district council were meeting and talked with councillors on what, I imagine, was their favourite topic. This was what one termed the blight of conservation: the stultifying effect of too rigid an adherence to planning edicts about old buildings. Some of the villages had specific development plans in which what could and could not be done were clearly defined. Where these plans did not exist there was often confusion, resulting from an insistence on the preservation of that which was not worth preserving.

Thus an example was cited in which the planning authority had insisted on the preservation of every slab roof made of Teesdale stone. These were mostly very old, direly in need of repair and—to give an idea of the dimension of the problem—there were 120 in Barnard Castle alone. Not only were they terribly expensive to replace or repair, but craftsmen to do these and other similar jobs were proving impossible to find.

The whole problem had a vicious-circle twist about it, for as the average age in the villages gradually grew higher, resistance to change became more entrenched and this resistance was too often encouraged by the planning decisions that seemed incapable of variation. There was a despair among the people who had tried to effect certain changes in the venerable hamlet of Whorlton. But they soon gave up trying. Their ambitions in this direction were made to seem vandalistic: "Like putting a moustache on the Mona Lisa".

So, leaving the planners and the progressive councillors to their private war which has so much public consequence, I left for Middleton, and other points to the west. Straightaway I came upon a mystery.

I

This is at Middleton, the capital and focal point of the Upper Tees, and it strikes the visitor who dwells a while and who therefore gives the village more than a cursory glance. Many travellers intent on recording their experiences have passed this way over the years as they journey the whole length of the Tees from Cross Fell to Middlesbrough. Usually they have extolled the delights of the dale which are quite remarkable: greener and grander than those of Weardale, smiling where Weardale, to be fanciful, may be said to frown. The villages of Teesdale, particularly in its lower reaches, are far prettier; they tend to group round greens with gracious houses of a modest antiquity whereas the villages of Weardale, as we have seen, are linear, and usually contain little communal atmosphere.

The approach to Middleton from the heights of the upper Tees, indeed, has none of the grimness so widely evident in Weardale. The hills are less oppressively close and infinitely greener and whereas, as we have noted, the cottages and farmsteads on the hills of the Wear so blend with the brown of the surrounding countryside as (at times) to be virtually unnoticed, those in Upper Tees are washed in a pristine white. On a day of sparkling sunshine the effect is almost as striking as the white houses of the Mediterranean. This white on green is at once gentler and gayer, and even on a day of lowering wind and rain gives a calculated lift to the spirits which is enhanced by the courtesy one received at the tiny hotel at Langdon Beck. From here the walkers spread out on the fell paths and they make especially for Cauldron Snout. Here the Tees, after flowing in the manner of lake-like expansion for a couple of miles suddenly turns into a gorge or 'snout' (a marvellous word) and leaps furiously down a giant rocky staircase. This is the division between Durham and Westmorland, and in my opinion is a more satisfying cascade than High Force which one rapidly approaches as Middleton draws near. The story, incidentally, of those white farmhouses is that an eighteenth-century Duke of Cleveland (the title is now extinct) was out hunting when he became separated from his friends. As night was descending and the times were lawless he approached one of the houses which he thought he owned and demanded lodging for the night. But the woman of the house, alone since her man was out on the fells, slammed the door in the face of the Duke. The times, indeed, were lawless and she was not prepared to trust a stranger, however finely spoken he might be. So the Duke angrily had to turn away, vowing vengeance upon the cottager. He returned next day with the agent—to discover to his chagrin that the property belonged not to him but the Earl of Strathmore. Thereafter he vowed that his property should all be whitewashed to distinguish it from that of all the other property. The white-washing tradition is continued by the Duke's successor, Lord Barnard.

High Force, the first waterfall in England is always a fine spectacle, though Nathaniel Spenser, writing his *Complete English Traveller* in 1773, seemed somewhat unnecessarily overawed. His description is worth quoting: "A few miles west of Barnard Castle, the water of the river, having collected itself together at the top of a frightful precipice, falls down with such a prodigious force that it is heard at a great distance, for the perpendicular is twenty-three yards. The force of the water dashing against the rocks fills the mind with horror, but the scattered rays of the sun shining through the misty particles, gives the whole the appearance of a beautiful rainbow. The whole scene is so amazingly delightful that the spectator is lost in admiration at the infinite wisdom of the Creator of the Universe, and filled with the most elevated notions of His power and majesty.

"Those who have had the opportunity to see the cataracts of the Nile in Upper Egypt, and the Niagara Falls in America, will have their memories refreshed by visiting this place, and those whose stations in life hinder them from travelling in foreign countries to visit these natural curiosities will see them all here in epitome. . . ."

The modern traveller, less impressed maybe, still finds High Force a fine sight, especially in spate when the concentrated fury of the water is surely unique to England. The main torrent of the water cascades between the central rock and the Yorkshire bank of the river and in normal conditions it is easily possible, and I did it, to scramble from the Durham bank to this rock and gaze cautiously down from above the torrent. Cloudbursts are said on rare occasions suddenly and prodigiously to increase the water flow on the Durham side. Years ago two men were trapped on the central rock by this sudden rise of water. Attempts to rescue them were made by throwing a rope and one man escaped in this way. On the second attempt the rope snapped, and the body of the man was not recovered until after it had hurtled several miles downstream. The irony was that the man would have been perfectly safe on the central rock waiting for the floods to subside since it was not covered by water. In appalling flood conditions, and in cases of extreme rarity, the merging of the waters over the central rock is said to occur, though despite widespread enquiry I have met no one who has witnessed this spectacle or has known anyone who has.

But to return to the mystery of Middleton which obtrudes as soon as questions are asked. It concerns not the present but the past. Where, why, when, how? Ask—and in Weardale there was a glut of answers so that the social history of the people easily emerged. Ask at Middleton and there is usually a silence as though the village was suspended in the animation of the present without much consideration of what went before. A sort of episodic history, as we shall see, does transpire but it derives from a dozen sources, concerns a few picturesque characters, and is without cohesion.

This is a curious phenomenon since Middleton, with a population of 1,600 people, a bank, two doctors, a good hotel, a few pubs and an exultantly prosperous working men's club (as an unlikely amenity) is the place to which people from a dozen small villages and hamlets naturally gravitate. It is the centre also of an area officially categorized by the Countryside Commission as of outstanding natural beauty. Although thankfully the blight of the caravan is not so evident as in Weardale, the village fills up with tourists each weekend in summer and there is, at times, almost a metropolitan air of being busy—this, despite a physical isolation which, in a social sense can have many disadvantages.

With such an atmosphere, therefore, of being established, and with the signs of oldness all around one in the whitewashed houses of the village street, and the antique cobbled steps to the village church, one anticipates a proliferation of facts and figures about the last few hundred years of the kind so freely available at Gainford further down the Tees, for example, where a distinguished history has been written. There, or at Barnard Castle (where documented history presses upon one) or even at Cockfield or Staindrop where the local historian has been both busy and successful.

But at Middleton? One can find references, it is true, in Hutchinson and Surtees, but they are casual and generally uninformative. A rare volume, *Upper Teesdale Past and Present*, written by James Backhouse and published in 1896 apart from a word or two about the church, and the headquarters of the London Lead Company (then established in the village) is singularly reticent. The more modern pilgrimage undertaken by Morris observes scathingly that "Middleton-in-Teesdale is a rather crude stone-built village that need not detain us. There is, in fact, nothing here to see except the church—and that has been rebuilt."

But, of course, there must be much more to the past of Middleton than that. Leslie Thompson had been rector in the village for twenty-five years when I first met him and an earnest enquirer into the past in his previous parish of Cockfield where he had written the local history. He had been indebted for much of his information to the parish strong box—that is the safe in the church in which, usually, in addition to valuables and parish registers, journals are kept.

It was the habit of his predecessors in his previous parish, and certainly the custom of eighteenth- and ninteenth-century clerics generally in the North to compile a record of their activities which were diverse indeed. These records they placed in the safe for posterity together with such impedimenta they had acquired in a useful life which (they supposed) posterity might cherish. There is no reason to suppose that the parsons of Middleton departed from this norm to any remarkable degree—at any rate until a Mr Milner became rector almost precisely a hundred years ago. Mr Milner, with a power modern clergy certainly do not possess, decided that the thirteenth-century church should be demolished and a decent Victorian edifice erected in its place. He proceeded to put this decision into practice, the walls of the old church proving so resistant that dynamite had to be used.

The new church was duly built but before it was complete Mr Milner died. Thereafter supposition takes over. It is the thought of Mr Thompson that the strong box deposited at the rectory during demolition and rebuilding, was cleared out by relatives of the rector at his death when they disposed of the personal clutter, possibly of centuries, leaving only the parish registers when the box was sent to the new church. So—no history, all tidy, which Mr Thompson in his twenty-five years in the village he had grown to love deeply, would have been so pleased to record in narrative form.

But history, of a shadowy yet deeply personal form does emerge, and, so far at least as I could discover, it is enshrined in the names of Jacob Readshaw, Dick Watson, Tom Todd and a man named Lee.

But first of all this 'new' church of St Mary the Virgin, built on the site of the old one in 1876. It has a separate bell tower of the sixteenth century, and the east window of the old church now stands somewhat dramatically alone in the graveyard. It also has a strikingly beautiful oak reredos above the altar the subject of which is the Good Shepherd. This remarkable work brings up the name of Jacob Readshaw. He was the village boy who became a joiner's apprentice, then a cabinet maker, then a violin maker and finally a wood carver. It is said, but not absolutely proven, that this beautiful reredos is his work. He also was the village astronomer. He constructed his own telescope and ground his own lenses. He was also, almost incidentally, a painter, and the picture of the squat thirteenth-century old church in the vestry is his work.

However, if Readshaw added picturesqueness to the last decade of the nineteenth century, he was not the only one. There was Richards Watson, the rhymester of Middleton, whose muse was so active in such unpromising conditions, that he filled a packed volume (now very rare) with his whimsy. And this, it seems was only the discernable tip of his prodigious output. Mostly while at work in the lead mines he would "delight his fellow labourers with his witty effusions." These pieces of rhyme were produced mostly on demand, and for every one that was printed at least a dozen were verbal and vanished into the air as soon as they were uttered.

His *Poems and Songs of Teesdale*, which is to be deposited for future generations in the strong box at Middleton Church, contains mostly long narrative rhymes in praise of the local countryside. But like a Laureate he could also sing for his supper, sufficient, anyway, to compose a complex *Ode to The Jubilee of Queen Victoria*, but also in celebration of more mundane occasions. There is, for instance, the ode on the occasion of the opening of a local footbridge. He would drop a verse in gratitude for having been loaned a book, and could write sixteen stanzas on catching a rat in a trap. He is one of only two examples I have come across in all the villages of Durham of the genuine poetaster who would compose his verse as a dialogue or in if necessary a nearly incomprehensible dialect. For several decades no function at Middleton seems to have been complete without his presence to stand up and proclaim the occasion suitably. All his life he was grateful for the fact that, as the son of an employee of the London Lead Company he was sent, at the age of six, to the company school—a favour not usually conferred on working-class children in 1839. He stayed only until he was ten but it was enough. "For without those precious few years I would never have been able to put pen to paper," he said. "I would have felt so bitter and deprived that

I think I simply would have walked over the fells one winter night and never returned."

So if the verse of Watson reveals the ruderies and the joys of life in the village so long ago, the prose of Thomas Todd is equally frank. He was a lusty young man, apprenticed to his father who was the village blacksmith. His *My Life as I Have Lived It* written in 1935 when he was eighty-one (and also destined for the church strong box) talks of poaching in the 1870s and 1880s when there was an open and accepted warfare with the gamekeepers who would pepper you with lead if they caught a fleeting glimpse of your breeches. Tom moved into the licensed trade and became an inn-keeper: the first night he threw a troublemaker on to the street. He was over six feet tall, fourteen stones in weight, with arms like young oak trees. "I had to do it," he says explaining the rough handling, "just so they knew who would be master."

When he was very young he sat at the feet of his grandmother, a kindly, wrinkled old dame who lived to be eighty-eight. She had nine sons and two daughters. "How do you think I got them all their dinners, Tommy?" she asked him one day. "Well, they would eat a lot," he replied. "I boiled a great pan full of potatoes, mashed them well and stirred some milk in. I didn't have enough plates for all or enough stools for them to sit on. So I just set out the pan on the floor and gave each of them a spoon. 'Dig in,' I told them, and that's how they got their dinner."

Tom Todd did not remain an innkeeper too long, went back to his forge and was the village smith until he was eighty. Then he gave up because, as he apologetically observes at the end of his charming, homespun little volume, "I found that my right arm was losing its vigour. . . ."

As for the mysterious Mr Lee, he was a local artist who, seventy or eighty years ago exhibited in the Royal Academy. But where are any of his pictures today? A prolonged search for even one of them to hang in the church has met with nothing.

Middleton today is a community which, in truth, is as isolated as it very well can be in modern times—and this despite the week-end influx of tourists who scarcely affect the real lives of the natives. The village is twenty-five miles from Darlington and twenty-two miles from Barnard Castle, and otherwise is pretty well surrounded by the broad acres of Durham and Yorkshire. Employment for adults is minimal; this, therefore is obtained by commuting to the Glaxo works at Barnard Castle or in the diminishing number of quarries in the vicinity. Opportunities for young men, therefore, are few, and the number of them joining the Forces or otherwise freeing themselves from the strict confines of village life is too high for comfort. From all this there arises the concurrent problem of an ageing population, and a slight imbalance in the sexes. Thus marginally more girls are leaving the village on marriage than there are girls arriving from other places upon their marriages to local boys. Nobody would wish this trend to increase.

Of controversy there is plenty; it rages, then ebbs, and often centres on the question of amenities of which subject the villagers are especially sensitive. What, for example, to do with the Primitive Methodist chapel which was closed but cannot be pulled down because of a Conservation Order? The matter of the siting of a car park and a fire station has exercised and animated local minds, and the public meeting, called when opinion is really enraged, is (I was creditably informed) a heartening example of village democracy at work.

The problem in Middleton is the same, really, as it is at Gainford and Staindrop forty miles away at the lusher and prettier end of the dale. This quite simply is a consciousness that the old order in the village is changing. At the moment nobody quite knows whether the change might not be for the worse. For no one, remotely, is emerging nowadays like Readshaw, Watson, Todd or the mysterious Mr Lee.

Not long ago the honoured position of Clerk to the Parish of Gainford paid the princely sum of £5 a year and there was no shortage of applicants for the job. This was about the time when the maypole was in regular use on the village green, and when Mr Hornsby, a saddler, celebrated his twenty-five years of teetotalism (he having been saved from drunken ruin by joining the Band of Hope) by giving a tea on the green for the village children. I mention the green and the maypole at the outset of this brief sketch of what has repeatedly been described as the jewel among Durham villages to emphasize changing times, and to suggest a slight but perceptible tarnishing of the delectable image of this most delightful of villages.

Nowadays there are few takers for the post of Clerk to the Parish even though the rate for the job is £100. The modest prestige of the office, the fact that the incumbent was (and is) at the centre of village decisions is reckoned to be poor recompense for the bother and the chores which, in any case, are scarcely onerous. The maypole, of course, no longer stands; it would be romantic in the extreme to suppose that it would, though the green is as splendid as ever, and in the late spring when its sides are suffused with a mass of daffodil, it inspires a Wordsworthian flight of fancy.

But the impression which grows stronger the longer you remain in the village is that the true nature of its achievement belongs almost totally with the past, and that the traditional attitude to present-day life is one of mild regret that so much of the homely activity and 'gracious' living has gone. I have been in no village in all Durham where this impression has been so strong.

Perhaps these regrets are foolish but they spring from a consciousness that the village once so happy with its tight, corporate life is now the increasing home of commuters. Two new 'executive' estates (whatever that word may mean) are home for the young families whom, the traditionalists would claim, make a relatively small impact on village life. The row of new houses on the lower side of the green, though pleasant enough in themselves seem astonishingly out of place, being detached whereas the whole charm of the housing on this and on the other side is in the serenity of the eighteenth-century terraces. All this and a group of somewhat ill-favoured council houses indicate a trend of the present not precisely as many of the villagers would wish. Add to this an ageing population (a cry that goes up nearly everywhere), virtually no local employment, and the move of the senior children away for their schooling, and it is scarcely surprising that the changing of the old order, and all that this seems to imply to them, should so dominate the conversation of so many of the older indigenous population.

The truth is that though Gainford has considerable antiquity— its Saxon name was Geginford and is mentioned in the Hatfield Survey of 1375 as being a thriving hamlet "not molested or perturbed by the King's enemies"—its glory days were those in the eighteenth, nineteenth and first few decades of the twentieth century. Evidence of this is all around you—even its most noted (and for all I know) only murderer, George Lockey, who was hanged at Tyburn, was a Regency man. There is a history, too, of prosperity. There is no record in Gainford, and no memory among the old people either, of children of the poor going barefoot to school as was common in the less affluent villages and towns of Durham. This prosperity was reflected in other ways. In the middle nineteenth century, for instance, the village had five boot and shoe makers, three blacksmiths, two tailors, two butchers, and sundry ironmongers, chemists, druggists, grocers, drapers and spirit merchants—and all with the total population of something less than 1,000. Then, and later, the characters of the village are remembered and recalled with affection. The Hunters of Selaby Hall, for instance who kept eight grooms, and who would drive to the railway with postillions to board special trains for balls in Newcastle. People like Mrs Hardy, mother of eleven hopeful children who, to augment the family income, bought a mangle, established it on the green and mangled clothes for one penny a basket. The money she earned was paid, in turn, into the bank accounts of each of her children, and she walked into Darlington each Saturday morning for this purpose. Hard days, one supposes, but people contrived as most certainly did the village caterer who bought calico for tablecloths and afterwards gave it to her daughters to wash and use for their trousseaux. It was the habit at the turn of the century to pay farm workers £1 a week—but they happily contrived as well. Even with half a dozen children which he would normally have at a minimum he could manage comfortably enough for he also had his house and garden, sixty stones of potatoes a year and a pint of milk a day. The wife of the one I am referring to, and he was typical enough, also worked on the farm for a shilling a day from eight till five. The image of the village emerges compulsively as tightly clannish and happy with none of the unhappiness seen in early industrial Weardale. But in Weardale the industrial working-class was emerging. In Gainford it was still labourers, shopkeepers and gentry happily coexisting.

Nowadays if you walk around Gainford—and even the most untutored can do so with knowledge since Durham County Council have provided a splendid walkabout leaflet—the impression is all of serenely preserved Georgian and Regency charm. I have noted the out-of-place detached houses, but there's nothing of this nature, for example, in South Terrace where the three-storied eighteenth-century narrow houses are fine examples in their time. Similarly in High Row, so graciously curved, and composed of houses each with a distinct personality of its own. Doorways and porches are all different but the style is predominantly Georgian and the same materials are used throughout. One building destroyed here would radically affect the whole Row, but happily the prospect is remote.

They are all conserved—some of the most precious relics I have seen anywhere in Durham, and a tribute to the good taste of those prosperous Darlington shopkeepers who built them to enjoy their retirement. You can spend a whole morning prowling in High

Row, noting what many are ignorant of—that some of the houses
have fascinating and intimate courtyards at the rear, and gardens
with high stone walls. There is nowhere quite like this in the
county. Pick a morning when it is quiet and sunny; imagine one
or two ladies in bonnets and bustles and the old cliché about time
standing still is a cliché no more.

The rest of the village includes Gainford Hall, a fine restored
Jacobean mansion and, in the garden, the curiosity of a seventeenth-century dovecote with a beehive domed roof which supplied
the people at the hall with pigeons' eggs. Hall and dovecote are
specially preserved buildings. A little along the river towards the
smaller village of Winston is a contributory reason to the village's
eighteenth-century prosperity. This is Gainford Spa which is a
structure like a font in a pool at the river's edge and with a mineral
water fountain. Certainly in the eighteenth and early nineteenth
centuries people came to Gainford to take the waters, which were
described thus: "A sulpherous spring, resembling in quality and
sediment those at Croft and Dinsdale and much used by the
country people. It probably needs the sanction of fashion to be as
much frequented as those places; and the attractions of the neighbouring scenery are certainly inferior to neither of them." In the
event, Gainford has never really been a popular spa village, though
a number of boarding houses were built at one time for those taking the waters.

Meanwhile, and as always, the river Tees is the village's constant companion; you hear its ripple—or its rush at night from the
houses round the green. People fish for trout, picnic on the banks,
and swim, though it is not truly safe. The river, though, has not
always been so benign. In 1771 part of the village was flooded,
bridges were swept away, the churchyard was inundated, and the
flood resulted in the river changing its course so that some acres
of Durham land were freely presented to Yorkshire.

Perhaps the gift by the planners referred to at the beginning of
this chapter of those Yorkshire acres to Durham was somewhat
intended to repay old debts.

Further eastward still, though, and it becomes increasingly difficult to visualize such stern matters as flood and inundation, the
Tees becomes, quickly enough, a calm dignified river up to and
beyond Darlington, winding now prodigiously, around Pierce-
bridge, High and Low Coniscliffe and even more so at Croft (on
the Yorkshire side) Hurworth, Neasham, Sockburn and the appropriately named Middleton-One-Row. Now there are no rock or

cascades; the river has still pools for anglers, and gently sloping green fields, in place of the towering hills each side of Middleton in Teesdale. There are gentle riverside walks and trees deeply encrusted with ivy lean out over the water. All this pleasance, is commuter land, and one reflects on how fortunate are those who work in Darlington, and within the throbbing technological muscle of Teesside—and can have the choice—if they have the means— of a dozen delectable retreats, deeply entrenched in quiet. A dozen? More like fifty villages and hamlets and each within half an hour by car from the metropolis of Darlington (itself worth living in now that main traffic passes it by) from the chemical complex at Billingham and the oil terminals and refineries of Middlesbrough.

Some like the exquisitely named Coatham Mundeville and Harrowgate are now no more than names just off the motorway as the A167 approaches central Darlington. It is worth recalling, though, that Coatham, belying its present suburban appearance is of considerable antiquity, deriving its name, it seems, from a Norman family, the Amundervilles, who took the territory over as part of the reward for aiding the conqueror. There is an old mill by the river (this is the Skerne, a tributary of the Tees) and this mill replaced a still older one at which flax was first spun by machinery in 1787. If one leaves the motorway earlier, but still within the orbit of the lower Tees, one chances upon Great Stainton which sits astride the old Roman road which used to surge northward in search of Hadrian's Wall. Stainton is typically without pretension; pantile-roofed cottages, the whitewashed 'King's Arms' (which thankfully remains unmodernized) a giant, dominant sycamore on the tiny green, a village pump enclosed in wrought iron in commemoration of the Queen's Jubilee in 1887, and the smoke of Teesside on the thankfully distant skyline. This is the backcloth; in the forefront on a drowsy summer Sunday afternoon, children play cricket, a young architect describes his desperate search outward from Teesside for a corner of land to build his dream house —ending here. He looks in the long grass for a lost kitten; the wood pigeon calls monotonously, and in half an hour only one car goes deeper into the remoteness of the even tinier hamlets of Bishopton and Redmarshall.

There is a somewhat brisker traffic, though, proceeding southward towards Sadberge which groups around the crossroads at the once busy road between Darlington and Stockton. Now, though, Sadberge is bypassed by the A66 a mile away, and seems more than ever a sleepy inconsequential hamlet, where nothing, conceivably, has ever happened—or even could.

History, though, tells a dramatically different story. Sadberge was very important indeed; it was a wapentake in the ancient Saxon kingdom, which means that it was the headquarters of a huge area of Northumbria. It had been also a centre of Roman military power and subsequently became an Assize town until the fifteenth century, when with the burgeoning power of the Prince Bishops, Durham grew in importance and Sadberge declined.

None of the old glory, of course, lingers now, and Sadberge is easy to miss. It is not picturesque; there is no church of glory or compelling tradition; no special reason for cars to intrude and villagers are thankful for this, though the two inns in the village, 'The Three Tuns' and 'The Buck Inn', would welcome more trade. Still, Sadberge repays those who meander around and ask a few questions. The vast conical stone on the green and under the shadow of several great trees, was established there (it is a relic of the Ice Age) in 1887 with a small plaque in celebration of the jubilee.

The Queen, after all, was Countess of Sadberge. You wonder why and discover a whole book written about Sadberge by Mr Lancaster Taylor, who was the rector from 1887 until 1911. A tremendous achievement, this, to write 280 pages when there was no documentation; no Surtees or Hutchinson bothered much with Sadberge which was as obscure in their day as it is today. Mr Taylor distills the essence of the quiet place of his time, but most of his Victorian prose, of course, has little relevance today. But the Queen, he reveals, is Countess of Sadberge because in 1836 the revenues of the Wapentake and Manor of Sadberge passed to the Ecclesiastical Commissioners and the honours attached therefore came to the Crown.

So far as the inns of the place are concerned, Mr Taylor is not enlightening; his teetotalism, it seems, was unbending. They are both places of a modest antiquity, the Buck Inn being named after George Buck a local philanthropist who created the Buck charities to buy blankets for the needy of the village and to give books to the village school at Christmas. The inn sign depicting a man with a bag of money duly commemorates this estimable gentleman though a tenant in the 1950s, perhaps predictably concluding that Buck referred to a rabbit, had a painting of the creature ready for hanging outside before the truth was angrily conveyed to him.

The Tees draws near now. On the junction of the A67 between

Darlington and Eaglescliffe there is Fighting Cocks, a centre for
the illicit sport in the eighteenth century, the site of a wire works
a hundred years ago, but now merely a junction *en route* to the
river. So to Middleton St George with the Teesside Airport nearby
and finally to the one street of terraced houses, the delectable three
star Devonport Hotel, and the Tees at Middleton-One-Row. From
a mullioned window of the hotel you can look down the steep
grassy bank to the river, see how placid it has become, so that even
the water lilies scarcely waver, and you become conscious that the
journey down the Tees is nearly done. No contrast with the heights
above High Force in a rain storm could be more decided than this.

The journey is nearly over—but not quite. Because though
further east there remain only towns and pollution, neither of
which need concern us, there is a need to retrace one's steps. We
have made the descent via Middleton and Gainford. Then, in trying a different approach through the antique lands of Stainton
and Sadberge a small central wedge of the river has been missed.
In this stretch the river bends more furiously than ever as we
approach Low Dinsdale which is quiet now and unimportant to
all those except the fortunates who live there. It had pretensions
for being a spa once since workmen discovered a sulphur well when
digging for coal. That was in 1789, and the Victorians, who had
a high regard for the curative powers of the Dinsdale water made
it, for a time, a populous place. But like Gainford; indeed like
Croft just on the Yorkshire side of the river, it missed becoming
a spa of national eminence precisely, one supposes because it was
so far away from the affluence of the South.

Now only fishermen sit on the broad river banks and there seems
no other activity at all. It is the same at Neasham which is a hybrid
village: new bungalows facing an old village street, and quickly
enough you reach the much bigger Hurworth, near now to both
Darlington and Yorkshire. It is a linear village, lovely with an extensive green, and as you approach the arched bridge it changes
its name to Hurworth Place—just, presumably, to confuse you.
There was a toll bridge here and a toll house which disappeared in
the Tees flood. There was also a nineteenth-century linen industry
and employment for 120 hand-loom weavers, all of which is gone
now. Only the commuters and the farmers remain. Finally there
are the Coniscliffes. At High Coniscliffe a traveller catching the
church and vicarage on their high escarpment above the river in a
snow storm and at twilight castigated it as "a miserable village
with a dead alive November aspect." I think he was much too

harsh and having, coincidentally, seen it in much the same garb, found the scene both eerie and fascinating. At Low Coniscliffe notoriety comes from the Baydale Beck Inn which, allegedly, was the rendezvous of many eighteenth-century desperadoes and, it is said, Dick Turpin made use of the inn. It is a nice thought, though I hasten to add that the area is the epitome, nowadays, of farming and commuter respectability.

So, what was there left of Teesdale? My journeys had been pleasantly diversified. It would have been logical, once Gainford was behind me, to step on briskly to Staindrop whose antique charm so closely matches Gainford's own. But I had been diverted by insidious voices whispering about Sadberge and Great Stainton. So here I was, Teesdale and its enchanting environs nearly done, and I had still not seen Staindrop.

In truth I had been there many times, but not, as it were, on a pilgrimage of finding out. To Staindrop, then, on the utterly final Teesdale quest, but first of all to Raby, and to gaze about me in some wonder in the Baron's Hall.

In 1569 when the Nevills, one of the most powerful families in the country, led the Rising in the North in a bid to return England to the old religion, 700 knights and their armour filled the Hall. It is a huge echoing chamber, one of the ninety-four rooms this most marvellous of castles possesses, but looking at it today one still wonders how they all squeezed in. One makes the obvious point to illustrate at the outset the sterling times Staindrop has lived through and to suggest the contrast, perhaps, with the quietude of today.

Staindrop and Raby are inseparable; it is inconceivable to think of one without the other. The village which is long, linear, and utterly charming, stretches out for more than a mile along the castle wall, and though nowadays, as we shall see, connections between village and castle are far less intimate than of yore, and the castle, sadly, is not inhabited by the Barnards any more, the influence it exerts is still profound.

But which came first? There is no doubt that Staindrop—it is the Danish name for a stony place—is of considerably greater antiquity than the castle. King Canute came this way on his religious pilgrimages and his mansion is thought to have been on the exact place which Raby Castle now occupies on the outskirts of the village. That there was a village here in the time of Canute there is no doubt.

In 1378 Lord John Neville was given a licence by the Bishop of

Durham to build the castle, though the Nevills had been at Raby in somewhat lesser magnificence since 1061. With the castle, though, their power multiplied prodigiously. The castle, according to Hutchinson, the most assiduous of Durham's historians was (at the end of the eighteenth century) "a noble pile of stately towers retaining all the appearances of its antiquity and giving the most perfect idea of a great baron's palace in the feudal ages." Thus it still is today. One can well imagine the overweening arrogance within the castle walls, the trepidation of the subject villagers of Staindrop and also the immense error which led to the failure of the rising and to the Nevills being stripped of their lands and fortune. This resulted in due course in the association—largely peaceful and wholly beneficial—between the ancestors of Lord Barnard and the village.

In 1570 when the rising had failed the ultimate in vengeance was wreaked on the Nevills. As I have just said, the castle and every possession was forfeited to the Crown. The leader of the family, Charles, the sixth Earl of Westmorland, fled to the Netherlands where the ruling Spaniards granted him a slender pension upon which he existed until his death in 1584 when the title became extinct. He had been convicted of high treason and outlawed in 1571. Raby and all the other Nevill estates remained with the Crown during the reigns of Elizabeth and James I. It was he who caused the manor and castle of Raby to be passed in trust to the citizens of London. In 1626 they were sold to Sir Henry Vane for £18,000 and they remain with his descendants to this day. Since then association between castle and village has nearly always been benign. The village scarcely changed at all between the end of the eighteenth century and the beginning of the 1914–18 war and it was at this period when the modern appearance of the village—small and elegant stone houses grouped round a series of interlocking greens—was settled.

Then the tight, corporate community of castle and village seems to have burgeoned and been most prosperous and happy. This is not to say that Staindrop is not a happy village today. But modern attitudes—as elsewhere—press hard upon it. Old people yearn, young people grow impatient. Simply it is not the same.

In 1698 the head of the Vane family had become Lord Barnard, and it is that name which is most honoured in Staindrop today. In the time of the tenth Baron—he died in 1964 and, at the time of writing estate duties had still not finally been sorted out—this association between castle and village most delicately and satisfactorily was maintained. His task was far from easy. He succeeded to the title in 1918 and he was the first of the line to feel the impact of modern times and rampantly changing ideas. But he was gentle, understanding, liberal, kind; yes he had all these virtues and needed them to preside over and live in a pile such as this, and to identify the villagers with what he was doing. He would climb the castle tower and survey the broad acres and the manor of Staindrop with a telescope. This was his harmless eccentricity and it never hid his obvious virtues or the great *rapport* he and the village enjoyed.

He was a great Scouter with an abiding love of children; those at the village school could count on his educational zeal. He was, among many other things an arboriculturist of distinction, and would give guided tours of his plantations to the more senior pupils. Once from his eyrie on the castle roof he spied the local schoolmaster trying—vainly—to drive stakes into the village cricket field which was situated within the castle walls. No vandalism was here intended: Mr Fred Blyth was simply desiring to mark off as protection the playing square before the children disported themselves in the school games the next day. Still, it was a fruitless exercise, and Lord Barnard descending quickly gave the reason why. Eighteen inches below the cricket field's surface lay the foundation of the township of old Raby, the medieval habitation of the serfs and vassals of the castle which only disappeared in the second half of the eighteenth century, so, of course, the stakes were foundering on solid rock.

There are some who wish that the dominion of the old lord could have continued for ever. They speak nostalgically—as you would expect—of those more expansive, less inflationary days. As late as 1941, for instance, there were nineteen men permanently employed on drainage in the plantations and twenty-one in the timber yard. Today there are no drainers and two men in the yard. That sort of comparison could be pursued almost endlessly. Instead of the 700 knights and their armour in the Baron's Hall alone there are now, throughout the whole castle on days when visitors are not admitted, only a couple of cleaners and a curator. The present Baron lives at the dower house a couple of miles from Staindrop, and the dowager lady in one of those splendid Georgian dwellings at Gainford.

Changed times indeed, but at least there are some constants: the herd of deer has roamed the parklands of the estate since 1190. Sometimes when they gather between the roadway and the castle,

particularly when the day is lowering and sunless, the scene somehow seems unchanging: as it was when the Nevills gathered for a
civil war that never came.

You walk from the castle gates to Staindrop Church in five
minutes. Here, as you would expect, the interior of what was
originally an eighth-century Saxon church is dominated by the
oak and alabaster effigies of the Nevill family, some of them very
ornate indeed. These, while undoubtedly they inspired a proper
awe in retainers in the past (and still attract church historians
from all over the world) provoked also a certain irreverence. One
of the most magnificent of the tombs, of a fifteenth-century
Nevill, has the feet of the effigy resting on a dog. Across the dog
there is roughly inscribed the words: "John Smith, school 1629."
A later vicar of Staindrop, Nathaniel Ward, writing in 1693, complained that he had to contend with impiety and barbarism. Perhaps he had in mind the vandalistic schoolmaster Mr Smith.

The village is surrounded by magnificent agricultural land and
is said, though I cannot explain precisely why, seldom to attract
a thunderstorm. It is relatively unaltered; there are no plans for
extra roads to be driven through, and the main road from Bishop
Auckland to Barnard Castle, which benignly splits both green and
village is looked upon as a boon by all except the most insular.
Old people in the alms houses, for instance, who have idyllic views
over open country at the rear, share these opinions, leave their
houses and sit in the village centre to watch the traffic pass by.

The houses on south green, which are substantially eighteenth
century, have gardens which are narrow but of inordinate length—
as much as 150 yards. These, as well as those on the north side
which end directly at the castle wall, were formerly tenanted exclusively by castle employees. In Victorian and Edwardian times
the stupendous gardens with, perhaps a cow and pig on tether,
made these servants, despite the tiny wages, largely self supporting.
They worked grindingly hard for their lord and for themselves.
There were only two statutory holidays—Christmas Day and Good
Friday. To this day the ceremonial day in the village for planting
garden potatoes is Good Friday.

The village has forty council houses and a few modern private
houses which almost totally escape your notice. The battle for
ownership of the village green, common in the past to almost every
village in Durham, has long since been won. A previous Lord
Barnard graciously conceded defeat, and now it belongs to the
villagers. Once a year, still, there is a carnival on the green, and the

quoits that they play, the greasy pole that they climb, and the rope that they tug, betrays a sense of yearning for some far simpler times, and boredom from others who believe—with only relative accuracy—that nothing ever happens in Staindrop. The activity of the village hall seems to belie this criticism, but the argument will continue. There are four pubs, eighty years ago there were sixteen. I was assured, however, that it was years since a drunken man was seen in the village and he, of course, would be a foreigner. The church has a magnificent peal of eight bells but in recent years has been without a team of ringers.

Like Gainford, and because of the kindly insistence of the Durham County Council, a leaflet guide is available showing that fascinating evidence of the past is not confined to castle and church. There is a unity of eighteenth-century building styles which would please the purist more if some of the houses at least did not suffer by the addition of Victorian bay windows. There is, if you look closely, a fine variety of fanlights, especially in the eighteenth-century houses, and there is a surviving example of an eighteenth-century blacksmith's shop which, throughout the nineteenth century and beyond, was a gathering place for the men of the village. It continually astonishes one to discover the number of specialist people villages like Staindrop used to contain. There has, for instance, been no substantial change in the population for 150 years. Then it was 1260; at the last count it was still 1240. Yet in the mid-nineteenth century this population provided employment for three ministers of religion, four doctors, two solicitors, one vet, five schoolmasters, two principals of ladies' academies, one auctioneer, one land surveyor, six grocers, three butchers, two booksellers, one druggist, three tailors, six boot and shoe makers, four blacksmiths, two saddlers, together with joiners, wheelwrights, painters, a clockmaker, and two millers and their mills.

Staindrop, finally, is the home village of a champion grower of sweet peas, and is so strictly governed by a Conservation Order that there is absolutely no danger of radical change through construction or demolition. It is, I think, the leading village of all Teesdale, though this is a title many in Gainford would dispute. No matter, they are not twins, but closely of kin, each handsome and elegant, somewhat browsing in the past, somewhat worried and mystified by the present. But, withal, they are both places of serenity, and this is their greatest virtue.

I left Staindrop, the Teesdale excursion virtually over, being recommended only to go back to my own kind of civilization via a hamlet or two: Ingleton, Summerhouse and Bolam. Each is remotely agricultural and impresses only in the paucity of the hospitality offered. Perhaps it is unfair to compare the small hamlet here with, for example, those in Devon, Dorset, Hampshire. I was thinking only of the pubs which, together with the cricket teams, interest me most strongly. I could not find a pub in Bolam; that at Ingleton produced a doorstep sandwich which I struggled unsuccessfully to master despite a healthy appetite while at Summerhouse the discomfort was acute. I wish the casual traveller was better served in the villages of Durham. The simple truth is that he is not.

12

Two Lovely Villages

NORTON is unique. There is no place in the northern counties, nowhere, certainly in Durham, that equals its precise combination of virtues or is more unexpected to the eye. There are faults about Norton, ways in which—ideally—it could be improved, but the best yardstick to assess the enviable image it conveys to the modern world is the reaction Norton provokes from visitors— preferably affluent ones from the South.

A recent story here can be told of the descent of an eminent industrialist upon the Norton scene for luncheon. He was not, maybe, a very wise industrialist, being imbued with the sad misconception (held by an astonishing number of otherwise estimable people from the home counties) that the county of Durham was full of pit heaps, monosyllabic (or else militant) inhabitants whom conceivably were adorned with woad. He was in the North-east on an important mission which was to end, everyone hoped, in the establishment of a factory in an area of high unemployment. He came reluctantly, spurred on by the urgings and the profound financial inducements of the Department of Employment. His reluctance stemmed partly from his own belief in the crass nature of northern life, but also from similar feelings shared by key workers and executives who providing the decision was taken, would have to exchange life in Pinner (or wherever it was) for what they deeply feared was something grossly inferior somewhere in Durham.

The industrialist, after a morning looking at sites and specimen factories, arrived at Norton with his host, was taken into a Regency house with a dining-room facing the green and with a fine view of the duck pond, and sipping a superb dry sherry (and with antique furniture all around him) confessed himself both bemused and contrite. He did not know (but then it is not well known) that it was possible to live in conditions of high and countrified civilization such as Norton exultantly provides, and all this within a five minute car ride, or a fifteen minutes brisk walk from the office.

He considered his own sad commuting which even the balm of Rolls Royce and chauffeur could not render immune from constant irritants. He considered those executives and key workers who used, train, car and shoe leather (sometimes all in the same journey) to get to work. He concluded—I believe somewhere between the lobster soup and the exquisite brandy—that though they all could not aspire to life around the green at Norton or even live in any of the lovely houses in the adjoining High Street, the point about the lack of graciousness of life had adequately been refuted. The factory came to the North.

I do not exaggerate what is a true story, but in any case, battles of a similar nature have been won on far less realistic grounds. But the industrialist could have been far more sensitive, sophisticated or, indeed, sensible than he proved to be and still have been confounded. Norton has that effect on all sorts of people.

Whichever way you approach, the surprise is considerable. Down the now familiar A19 the turn at a roundabout in Billingham is raucous and unpleasant. A wrong move here sends you to shipyard or iron foundry or some vast chemical complex. All is aggression and petrol fumes and money making. But a few hundred yards on the right road, the correct turning at Norton Church and in literally ten seconds the transformation is both dazzling and complete. I first took this road on a silent, snowy day in winter at dusk. Past the church, the village green, extensive, criss crossed by narrow roads, unfolded. The duck pond (no ducks nowadays) was frozen and early moonlight played on the ice. The old schoolroom in the centre of the green was lit up, and the lovely houses in a sort of ellipse round the green were distinct enough to appear individual, but enhanced by the vague beguiling light so that a little mystery was added. Someone walked a dog on the green, and the doors of one or two of the houses opened emitting a warm yellow glow. Ahead of the green were the lights and the bustle of the High Street, with its old houses on one side, and shops of both character and distinction on the other. It was beneficence indeed, remembering the motorways and towering cranes and cooling towers, eternally steaming, which were just round the corner.

Round another corner you penetrated the proper environs of Stockton on Tees. Industry, dross and dereliction took over on one side; municipal ordinariness on the other. Norton—astonishing Norton—which should have been absorbed decades ago by rampant suburbia, remained utterly distinctive and delightful in the middle.

I last saw Norton on an afternoon in the middle of a 1975 heat wave. The duck pond resounded with splashing children; the green seethed slowly with languishing picnic groups; elderly people, mute and immobile, crowded the seats in every arbour and tree-protected avenue, and the mature red brick of the old houses glowed in the hot sunlight. I was taken through wrought-iron gates to the walled garden at the rear of one of these dwellings, classical early Victorian at its finest, and here, of course, with roses and wistaria clinging to the walls, and drinks in a shaded court-yard, the years fell away and even the centuries did not seem to matter.

Norton remains, if not a village as it used to be, remarkably preserved and inviolate, but then it has always been a fortunate place largely, I think, because in the past it was protected by the influential people who lived there, and now assiduous planners, understanding local authorities, and alert little pressure groups ensure that vandals of whatever age and outlook keep well away.

A child swinging on a tree branch will bring a householder to remonstrate; a youth carving initials on a seat may find the police suddenly present. A developer deviously seeking advantage discovers that his ploys are combated at every turn. There is not a better protected place in the kingdom than Norton. It was a Saxon village, then Norman, presented for deeds of loyalty to the Conqueror, and once named Normanton. It grew always in influence attracting the prosperous from Stockton just as other fine places on the Tees—Gainford is an example—profited from the attentions of the shopkeepers of Darlington.

It was, even in the eighteenth century, so desirable a place in which to build a dwelling that a piece of land adjoining the green was sold for £350 an acre. Always it has been a place of boarding schools for young ladies, and the homes of other genteel occupa-tions, and though in the eighteenth and nineteenth centuries there were very few shops in the High Street, it housed eight public houses and a couple of breweries. It acquired a reputation for be-ing the garden of Stockton because of its favourable soil and rural aspect. There is a story, indeed, that the potato was first intro-duced into Durham at Norton, and that the man responsible was Thomas Baker, farmer and Quaker preacher, who was known, per-haps predictably, as Potato Tom. He was totally illiterate but had a nice feeling for the spoken metaphor, and when in the pulpit occasionally scourged his flock for observing that they—some of them at least—were like the potatoes of the year: under a fair exterior they concealed a rotten heart. Another such idiosyncratic character of the period was Jeremiah Moore, a gentleman of extreme affluence who in his earlier life had escaped from Turkish slavery and came to riches when his brother, the Squire of Norton, died. When Jeremaih himself died he bequeathed his considerable fortune to the six who had befriended him in adversity, and they were handed their legacies at his handsome house on the green while partaking of a massive bowl of punch.

The ancient history of Norton, of course, is deep and detailed and not, truth to tell, all that interesting. But one fragment not well known has an eerie ring about it and maybe deserves repetition. In 1172 King Henry II granted Flambard, then Bishop of Durham, powers to hold a market at Norton on the Lord's Day, much, it seems, to the outrage of the pious people of the village. Later in the year Henry was on his travels in the North when he was hailed by an outlandish person "redhaired and with crescent-shaped tonsure" which showed that he was a priest of the olden church which still held out against Romish innovations. The apparition (for he seemed like nothing less) warned the King "in the name of Christ and his mother, and John the Baptist and Peter" that no traffic or servile works should be done throughout his dominions on the Sabbath Day, this especially applying to Norton. It seemed, anyway, as if the King ignored this warning and therefore calamities thickened upon him. The profane market at Norton waned and fell away. Profanity, though, in its more modern sense has never been a Norton characteristic, though the more insular of its inhabitants, more deeply entrenched perhaps behind the barriers of conservatism, might profess to see more vulgarity than meets the most far-seeing eye of an invader such as myself. They point out that though outwardly Norton is as much a village as ever it was, its sense of being a relatively isolated and self-sufficient community has long since gone. They speak nostalgically of the times fifty years ago when the horse trams left the duck pond for Middlesbrough, when there was a pub—the 'Hambledonian'—and the village school in the centre of the green, when the house with the red blinds, long since pulled down, was a landmark, and when the High Street contained far fewer shops. But even they are forced to admit that the green was far less handsome then.

Photographs at the turn of the present century show it as virtually treeless and more than a little forlorn. The towering sycamores, mostly planted seventy to eighty years ago which now give the village such intense character, were puny saplings as Victoria's reign ended. The invasion of Norton from the rude outside—such as it is—took place in the 1930s with the development of a large council estate behind the High Street, and with coincidental private development to the south of the village. There have been further forays since the war—a ring road, more houses, and the green has been bisected by a further road. Yet none of this affects the place's essential character, and though there was a period in the 1950s and early '60s when the High Street seemed imminently about to be submerged in supermarkets, the worst never really happened.

The class of shop may not always meet high (and uncommercial) ideals, but genuine village emporiums still remain. The village is alive with jealous inhabitants; middle-class, community conscious, knowing expertly how to foil pretentious intrusion. They complain that they do not have a pub of character (the two I visited were suburban ordinary) but in combination with the Church Commissioners who are large landowners, a highly sympathetic local authority and the Civic Society, anyone seeking radically to change Norton's character would not have a chance. Nor is there much likelihood of any substantial change for with a motorway as protection to the east, and bounded by the railway to the north, there is not much anyone can do with Norton except to leave it uniquely and marvellously as it is. Though a few thousand less cars passing through each day would make it better still.

There was no very logical reason why Norton should lead me to Egglescliffe. Rather the reverse since there is no direct road or connection one with the other and, in addition, I had never heard of Egglescliffe. Eaglescliffe—well that was different, indeed it was most familiar. I had been stationed at Yarm on the Yorkshire side of the border, and had proceeded to Eaglescliffe and had no very pleasant memories of small factories, service establishments, and a group of houses which, I supposed, constituted the village. There was no special purpose therefore, in being urged to go there. My Norton friends were both helpful and patient in the face of what must have seemed the crassest of ignorance, but they also smiled inscrutably as they glanced at each other. Plainly I was not the first of their visitors who should have known of the hidden place that is Egglescliffe but, somehow had not. Also there was, it

seemed obvious, a cogent reason for mixing Eggle with Eagle, but
was it not best, my friends suggested, to go to Egglescliffe first and
then all, they promised, would be made clear.

"But," they added, "they are shrewd people in Egglescliffe, and
though welcoming visitors, do not want to be descended upon by
hoards of ill-advised ogling people. You must proceed along the A19
from Stockton until you have almost reached the old bridge at Yarm
which constitutes the Durham–Yorkshire border. Look for a turning which says Butts Lane. Turn here and continue into the village.
There is a signpost but it prepares one for a much grander turning
than the crevice in the roadside you ought to take. Thus the traffic
rushes by and the villagers are happy that this state of affairs
should continue. That way only those with a purpose or the good
manners and educated curiosity to ask questions find their way into
Egglescliffe. Don't you think that a good idea. . . ?"

Yes, of course I did, though I imagine that the matter would
be tidied up by the planners as soon as I had tempted fate by
writing this. But even if they have as I write these words, indicated
the gorgeous cul-de-sac which is Egglescliffe with arrows, neons
and in letters a foot high from the main road as well as from the
Eaglescliffe approach, it is still unlikely to achieve the notoriety
of being a calling place for coach trips. Your way through the
village is here blocked by the Tees; there is a single pub, 'The
Pot and Glass', satisfactory and attracting a fair amount of discerning outside gin and tonic trade, but in no way capable or willing of projecting a mass-appealing image. There is a village hall,
busy with all the amiable activity of the country, and a friendly
community, once almost totally agricultural, but now diluted as the
farmers, especially the Smiths at the manor, modernize and
mechanize and thus save labour. Once there was a cascading away
from village life; this was in the heyday of the cinema, and the
other delights of Stockton. But now, with the telly, the vast cost
and relative unreliability of the buses, the disenchantment with
the pictures, there has been a return to and a happiness with the
village you would not have got thirty years ago. It is as if (and
several villagers acknowledged this) the magic of Egglescliffe, the
remarkable change of tempo from the crashing A19 have been
seen for the blessing they are.

"Returning to Egglescliffe," said one villager choosing his words
with care, "is like returning to the womb." For my part it is as if
a curtain was pulled aside revealing, on my succession of visits,
silence, sunshine, wind in the trees, and desultory conversation.

The coach traveller, should he ever penetrate the spot would assuredly call Egglescliffe dead. I thought it marvellously removed from the present.

But why Egglescliffe and Eaglescliffe? What is the mystery of two villages, close to each other, with almost identical thoroughly confusing names? The answer is that until 150 years ago there was only Egglescliffe, which is at least Anglo-Saxon and probably had a settlement in times of pre-history. Then, at the time of the beginning of the Darlington–Stockton railway in 1825 they were planning a junction some two or three miles away, in the adjoining parish of Preston. It could not be known by that name for fear of confusion with Preston in Lancashire. Therefore it would be called Egglescliffe junction. But how did you spell the confounded name? A petty bureaucrat enacting the decision, wrongly instructed the junction signwriter. The first 'g' became an 'a'; Egglescliffe, thus, became Eaglescliffe. In due course, since houses and works tended to group round the early railway junctions a new village parted from Egglescliffe by the A19 duly was born. It was not the first time, though, that there had been confusion about Egglescliffe's name. A seventeenth-century parson went through the parish register for centuries meticulously changing the spelling to Eaglescliffe—and then his successor changed it back again.

How did the name arise? No one seems to know. Certainly it has never meant 'eagles' cliff'. The explanation of the Oxford Dictionary of Place Names which connects the puzzling 'Eggles' with 'ecles'—a church—is the most likely meaning. For a church has stood on the 'cliffe' or promontory overlooking the Tees since earliest times. The discovery in 1937 by diggers in the churchyard of five hand-made building bricks believed to be 1,200 years old provides almost conclusive evidence of an Anglo-Saxon settlement and a church from which the name of the village would be derived. Though this is probably the truth of the matter, the Rev. A. T. Dingle who was rector of Egglescliffe from 1904 until 1935 reckoned to have discovered more than forty ways of spelling the name.

There is even a ballad written by another incumbent, Rector Brewster, in the early nineteenth century called *The Eaglescliffe Legend* which dwells romantically on the domain of the eagle. Mr Dingle says that this is the purest of fiction.

For a place so tiny there seems to have been an enormous amount of recorded history, though this, as we have seen elsewhere, probably arises because Egglescliffe is fortunate in having a succession of rectors who were assiduous in the records they kept.

By far the most remarkable of these characters was the afore-mentioned Rector Brewster, the author of an authoritative *History of Stockton*, the second edition of which he revised while living at Egglescliffe. Proud, arrogant, insular—so insular, indeed, that in his *History* he gives only a passing and casual reference to the Stockton and Darlington Railway, the first passenger railway in the world, which had begun operations only four years before and which, in effect, almost intruded on his doorstep. He came to Egglescliffe in 1814 and his coming coincided, so it is said, with a new lease of life for the village. Before that, and at least until the Napoleonic wars, the village was sunk in what was described as a medieval lassitude. Bonaparte's successes, though, stirred the village and made the people fearful. In October 1803 when in-vasion seemed to be imminent, plans were at hand to evacuate the village should Napoleon land at Teesmouth. When victory finally was won, the Egglescliffe people congregated at the bridge at Yarm to cheer the Duke of Wellington as he made his way to Stockton, and then to be a guest of the Duke of Cleveland at Raby Castle.

Stirring days, but unsettling, too, as Rector Brewster was wont to observe. In his *Thoughts on Residing in Villages* published in 1820 he deprecated the excitement and *avant garde* ideas which were rampant following the French Revolution. Pernicious prin-ciples were abroad—even in Egglescliffe. Farmers were falling from the plain and homely ways of their fathers. They had extravagant ideas about furniture and dress and the women, he bemoaned, were given to "tinsel follies". He bewailed the non-observance of the Sabbath, condemned the secular talk both before and after Divine Service when, it seems, his reluctant congregation were apt to discard piety for discussions on rates, road repairs—"and such temporal matters."

But though the invading Wesleyans and Primitive Methodists (whom he also deplored) might constantly be reminding the traditional Rector Brewster that religious observance was chang-ing, he did record one resounding success. This was his Sunday School which gathered in the ragged multitude who previously had played all Sunday by the well-sides and hedges.

Stirring times, indeed, but earlier, they had been of a different and bloodier nature. During the Civil War Egglescliffe was a Royalist stronghold largely owing to another remarkable Rector, Dr Isaac Basire. But after the battle of Marston Moor which gave the Parliamentary army control of the North he had to remain in hiding, eternally hunted by Cromwell's troops until he was able to join Charles I at Oxford in 1646. During part of that time, it is said, he hid in Egglescliffe, and when the village filled with searching troops he retreated to his last bastion, the old, now demolished rectory, and in a secret recess in the highest storey (and hidden by a sliding panel) he remained while the soldiers foraged unavailingly below. As might be expected, the bridge has insinuated itself into the lives of the Egglescliffe people in quite a dramatic way. The people of the early nineteenth century, often and unwittingly the vandals of ancient things, had plans to pull down the ancient structure which separates the parish of Egglescliffe from Yorkshire, and the cast-iron and monstrous structure which was to succeed it, was constructed at a cost of £8,000. It was about to be opened officially when, at midnight on 13th January 1806, it collapsed into the river. A night or two before, two businessmen from Yarm had driven on to the bridge in their carriage, and drank to its success in a bowl of punch. "May this bridge stand the test of ages till time is no more." Instead the old bridge was repaired and widened, the work being finished in 1840 and remains to this day.

Egglescliffe had (indeed still has) a reputation for gardens and orchards, it being the eccentric habit of one orchard owner to climb into the branches of his trees in spring when the blossom was out, surround himself entirely with foliage, and there pray that the frost might not spoil the fruit crop.

Various other eccentricities persist into contemporary life, one of which is a belief in a ghost said to manifest itself in the guise of a hooded monk at the rectory, but there is nothing either eccentric or mythological about Egglescliffe's reputation for longevity, since the voluminous parish records abound in examples of the villagers' profound ability to survive. The record for Egglescliffe and indeed for anywhere I have been in Durham is held by George Peacock, a farm servant of Aislaby. It was said to be the wonderful air and the placid days that helped him live to be 138.

13

Sedgefield: Fiction and Fact

I BEGAN this book enveloped in the exquisite melancholy of an autumn day: the leaves swirled and parachuted upon the roof of my parked car at Monkton when melancholy, as the opening chapter, I hope, makes clear, became a burgeoning, overwhelming emotion, because of the remembrances of things past.

Now the story is almost told and it is autumn again. The precise journeys, if I cared to trace a line from one place to the other, would make an impossibly intricate hieroglyph: steps retraced a dozen times; six day-long journeys through Teesdale; Weardale, encompassed from winter to summer; dozens of days, thousands of miles, people incredulous that one may be presuming to write a book. People also contemptuous and kind: the first because of a pathological mistrust of the printed word, and a belief vehemently expressed that I would get things wrong. When I retorted, as I did, that the approach was subjective, that I could write in no other way, and that, maybe, wrong and right were incorrect judgements, the silence, as they say, was pregnant with disbelief.

But kindness and interest over-rode all this occasional hostility. A writer vies with the occasional appearer on television in the interest he arouses. You write? How do you ever find the proper words? How many words will you write? What? All those! Now, I have sometimes felt I could write a book: my family says my letters are a scream, but somehow. . . . You write? Now that is an easy task sitting at a desk, putting words to paper. Do you wait for inspiration? Sometimes in the night I think of a beautiful poem but in the morning I've quite forgotten it. You write? How I wish I could write, because I have had some wonderful experiences abroad, at Dunkirk, with the Partisans in Yugoslavia. And the girls I knew when I was young; the stories I could tell. . . . It's all in my head, you know, but I've tried to put it all down on paper and then, somehow, it doesn't seem right. You write? So will I some day because there's that novel which will just be a saga of ordinary life. When I've time. . . .

Most people, of course, were not like this at all. They were briskly helpful: they would stop the business of the day and gravely consider the inscrutable problem you had suddenly presented to them: why the cottages in Teesdale were painted white, why the cricket field had disappeared, and how, more philosophically, they would relate regrettable historical happenings to the turbulence of the present day.

So it went on, weekend after weekend: the county traversed in all weathers and moods, for there is no other county in England, I think, where the contrasts are so profound and where beauty and aridity are so close.

As I went on my way, inconsequentially at times and at others to a stern plan, I frequently came close to, but never actually intruded upon one of the most interesting villages of all. Early on, in my pitmatic excursions, Sedgefield was on my doorstep, and in later days, as I sped down the motorway towards Teesdale, Sedgefield was merely a minute from a slip road. One hot Sunday afternoon taking an old Roman road to the Tees I was actually in its outskirts. Yet I sedulously avoided Sedgefield, largely, I think, because of a myth of childhood. It was associated then, almost exclusively in my mind with mental derangement. At Sedgefield there was a mental hospital and people, less concerned then with the niceties of expression referred to it badly and cruelly as a lunatic asylum. Someone "not quite right" (and they tapped their forehead) had gone to Sedgefield, the assumption being that he or she would never emerge. I may have been unduly sensitive but stories of this nature on which old dames would thrive were harrowing experiences. I would adorn the words in my imagination so that Sedgefield took on the misty aspect of a sinister place. It needed only an acquaintance somewhat older in years to be sent to Sedgefield and the horror in my mind became both coherent and lasting.

Thus for years I shuddered at the name as though, somehow, the hospital was some adult Dotheboys Hall which it is not and never was. And the village, of course, achieved the aura of barely mentioned things. I never in my childhood knew someone who actually lived there, nor did I visit the place until the day of rationality was with me (I hope) to stay.

But if Whitburn, because of its splendid cricket field, was associated with delight, Sedgefield was a bit like being forced to rest in a darkened bedroom when one desperately wanted the light.

Thus, as I traversed the county Sedgefield (I confess foolishly) was relegated to the end of the awesomely long list of places I still must visit. As I proceeded, and, ticking names from that list, also discovered yet more places that demanded attention, I considered fleetingly whether Sedgefield might not be ignored altogether. After all it would be in good company. I had never pretended, nor would it have been possible, to visit every village. Also there was another reason (so I argued by now capable of convincing myself about anything) and that was the doubt as to whether Sedgefield was a village at all.

Certainly it was a place of great antiquity; it had varied, not only in style, image and attainment, but also in what it was called.

There it was, anyway, between Durham and Teesside. Hutchinson, the eighteenth-century colossus, without whom any earnest enquirer into the state of Durham County would feel inadequate, described Sedgefield in 1821 as having one of the finest situations in the county standing proudly upon a swell of gravelly ground, open to every aspect, and remarkable for the health and longevity of its inhabitants. It was the abode in those days of more than one centenarian. A tribute to the salubrity of the Sedgefield climate was also paid by an imaginative gentleman, Dr Askew, who apart from being a well-known Harley Street physician in the eighteenth century also had the ready phrase for most occasions. He called Sedgefield the Montpelier of the North, apparently because the quality of the air reminded him of his honeymoon at that resort in the South of France. The comparison may seem eccentric, but the fact is that Dr Askew constantly urged his convalescent patients to stay in the village, and gave the quality of the air as his reason. He waxed almost delirious in Sedgefield's praise. "All the country round about," he said, "is in a high state of cultivation. The views to the south command a delightful view, down to the Tees and the German Ocean. . . ."

But all this time a great uncertainty persisted: was Sedgefield a town or a village? In 1823 Surtees, perhaps almost the ultimate authority, referred to Sedgefield as "a small, neat market town with the appearance, rather, of a handsome village." This is perhaps the crux of the matter, for though Sedgefield, by virtue of its medieval grant of a market, deserves the appellation 'town', such a description has never found any favour—at any rate until recently—with those who live there. The people of Sedgefield, canvassed recently by researchers from the University of Durham and the Work-

Staindrop, in the middle of rich farming land

Sedgefield, equidistant between Durham and Stockton

A pithead scene

A typical Durham Social Club

Two faces of Durham

Norton: (*above*) the green and duckpond (*below*) gracious houses

Two noteworthy pubs

The Buck Inn at Sadberge

"The Seven Stars" in Shincliffe

Leek growing: the Durham pitman's pride

ers Educational Association, agreed, almost unanimously, that it is as a village that Sedgefield should be known.

Yet, what confusion there is today! Notwithstanding local sentiment the parish council decided a year or two ago that henceforth the village should be known as a town, that they should therefore elevate themselves to the status of town council and that the parish council chairman, thereafter, should be distinguished by the title of mayor. That is the way it is now, and confusion is worse confounded by the additional reorganization of local government. This means that the offices of the Sedgefield District Council, previously sited in a Queen Anne building in the village (town?), have now been removed to the town of Spennymoor some miles away. It requires the exercise of some ingenuity nowadays not to mention the forbearance of Job, to determine which local government services are executed by the town (that was a parish), which by the district, which by the county authorities from Durham City, and which require consent from central government. This problem, apparent almost everywhere I went, is here crystallized, and made to seem as idiotic as assuredly it is.

If all this accounts, at least occasionally, for the bemused expression to be encountered when officialdom of any sort is canvassed for information, it has not notably affected the lives of the villagers (townspeople) who seem content in the knowledge that Sedgefield is a very prosperous, not to say booming place.

It used to be known as Ceddesfeld, Seggefeld or Segesfeld, general opinion being that the ancient name was derived from the fact that 'secg' was the old English for warrior. A more mundane theory is that it means simply the field of the sedge, being a reference to the marshy character of the area.

The old name has now been attractively revived since the council, having taken over the old Regency rectory and transformed it into a community centre, held a competition to find a name for the place and awarded the prize to the person who suggested Ceddesfeld Hall.

At first sight, and at any rate to the newcomer, Sedgefield does not suggest itself as a place that has undergone, survived or endured profound social change but this, indeed, is no more than the truth. When its name loomed ominously in my mind in childhood it was a sleepy market village equidistant between Durham and Stockton and lying astride the road from one to the other. It had and, of course, still has, a pleasant array of late seventeenth- or eighteenth-century buildings with a little extension into the nine-

L

teenth century and the Edwardian period. The Manor House, which is the fine example of Queen Anne architecture previously referred to, happily dominates the centre of the village and now operates as a magistrate's court. In the grounds of the old rectory and now jealously preserved are the turkey oaks—or at least three of the original five trees planted from seed by the brother of John Gamage who was Rector of Sedgefield from 1728 to 1748. The brother was a turkey merchant which is why the oaks are so named. They are massive and, even in Surtees' time, so he records, each had a girth of more than six feet. There are other old houses with names pleasantly evocative of vanished days: Badger's Green, an amalgam of three seventeenth-century cottages, The White House from the 1890s and then, of course, Sedgefield's only noble home, Hardwick Hall.

There was a manor house here in the fifteenth century but the present building is fairly undistinguished Georgian. The interest these days lies in the somewhat curious history surrounding the building since the estate was purchased by John Burden in 1748. His landscaping of the grounds was typical of the times: extravagant, including artificial lake, sham ruin, a bath house, temple and banqueting house, not to mention a pseudo-Gothic hermitage. All this apparently was a great attraction for the nineteenth-century tourist, but by the early days of this century had fallen into sad disrepair. Apart from the removal of the great staircase, the hall and its accessories, though increasingly decrepit, remained intact, though securely locked from the outside world throughout the '20s and '30s. It was then in the charge of Harry Peacock, a gamekeeper who is chiefly remembered for the hook attached to the stump of one arm which he had shot off himself while climbing a wall. Hardwick Hall, thereafter suffered much contemporary change, some of it vandalistic. Lead was taken from its roof to further the war effort; it became a hostel for Bevin Boys and then a maternity hospital. The rather grand front to the old banqueting hall was taken in 1947 to form the façade of a local cinema and (since the cinema has now become a clothing factory) has vanished completely. Much of the grounds which were Burdon's pride were sold for development and Hardwick Hall is now a hotel selling, I can testify, a particularly delectable local brew.

The centre of the village is pleasantly broken up by the green, now segmented by roads, with the thirteenth-century church of St Edmund the dominant feature. It is only a few years ago since they ceased tolling the curfew, and a relatively short period (the turn of the present century anyway) since it was the habit to fence in the green to discourage visits from vulgar fair people.

Much before all this, though, we find that Sedgefield was seething, as was so much of the North, at the consequences of the Reformation. There is no record, as there is at so many other places, of the people rising in arms, but in 1569 they did set up a high altar in the church, brought in holy water and said the Mass.

Then the Queen's soldiers came in, carried the sacred books to the stone cross in the centre of the green and burnt them, returning to the church to smash the altar. These incidents apart, facts about the remoter history of the village are almost impossible to track down, none of the historians of the eighteenth and nineteenth centuries, so assiduous almost everywhere else in Durham, having much to contribute. There is a little more to be added about the nineteenth century where the picture that emerges is one of solid respectability. Eminently it was a charitable sort of place there being twenty-five registered charities and the Durham County Asylum, which aroused such terror in my childish heart, was certainly a place of light and sympathy—although there were passing scandals. It was built in 1857 and towards the end of the century was holding a huge number of patients, reports suggesting that they were largely left unattended at night, the staff of nurses having retired after a fourteen-hour day. There seems to have been some sensation here, for an exposé was written in true nineteenth-century radical style by Mr Thomas Dodds, editor of the shortlived *Sedgefield Ratepayers' Journal*. However the passing of a Mental Health Bill opened many locked doors, cleared away some abuses, and notorious 'attendants' largely disappeared. I imagine that it was memories of sad days before the Bill was passed, handed down through the generations which caused the old dames to whisper so furtively when Sedgefield was mentioned. Nowadays, of course, as the Winterton Hospital, it pioneers the treatment of many forms of mental illness and is a repository of much enlightenment.

Sedgefield is a distinguished centre for racing, there being thirteen meetings a year, and a happy meeting place for nearly two hundred years for the South Durham Hunt. Addiction to the joys of the hunt apparently knew no bounds, and they were exemplified by one Mr John Harvey, Master in the 1860s. He was a tobacco merchant in Newcastle and three days a week he used to mount a hack at seven in the morning, ride thirty-five miles to Sedgefield and once there ride one of his four horses to hounds for much of the day. Then he rode back to Newcastle.

'The Hardwick Arms', still in the main street, used to be the coaching inn in the late eighteenth century, and with the coming of the railway Sedgefield found itself on the Stockton–Ferryhill line and in need of a station. However the convenience of the villagers was the last matter to receive consideration, Squire Ord who then ruled the village deciding that the 'abomination' should be at least a mile and a half from the village centre. This was in 1833, and the decision brought a healthy trade in transporting the passengers to the station. In the later years of the nineteenth century you would go by horse bus for sixpence.

All this time, of course, and, in fact, since the thirteenth century, they had been playing their curious game of football each Shrove Tuesday. The parish clerk was obliged to provide a small football, hand stitched out of saddle leather, and sides of an indeterminate number ranged over and out of the village, generally in the rough direction of assigned goals, but not taking too much heed of either these or any other rules. In practice the commotion usually moved quickly from the village and could become somewhat desultory. In the latter half of the twentieth century, however, and as a sign of the social revolution which I referred to earlier, the contestants have been handicapped by all sort of inhibitions their ancestors never dreamed of, notably traffic. In a recent year the game coincided with a miners' strike; young miners from far away converged on the village and vandalism and nuisance was rife. The next year the game was cancelled and there is virtually no demand that it should be revived permanently.

Finally the modern Sedgefield is being changed out of recognition because of two fortunate situations. The first is the building and opening of the by-pass. Before this splendid happening the village bisected the main road from Durham to Stockton and persecution of the inhabitants by fast cars and huge chemical lorries made life quite miserable. Now you can walk about in relative comfort, the pubs are packed and the shops prosperous. I can think of a few villages in Durham—Birtley springs to mind and every, straggling, linear place in Weardale—for whom such a by-pass would be similar boon.

The second facet of change is more gradual, its benefits are more imponderable and more hotly debated. This is the rise in population—and the reasons for that rise. In the decade and a half or so from about 1960, the population which had been stationery at about 2,500 for an age has increased to 5,000. This has come about because of the discovery by the young executive from Teesside that Sedgefield is a nice place—as well as convenient—in which to live: almost within sight of the steaming towers of the chemical industry, and the belching smoke of steel, despite being deeply rural. If he could not chance upon an individual house in a hamlet (and these have been beyond price) then the career technologist who might only be in Durham on a prolonged visit, was happy to settle for Sedgefield. Thus estates of more or less tasteful private houses have grown up on the edge of the village much to the concern of the conservatives and those too set in their ways. Their fear—that the village's character would be radically altered—was not necessarily totally irrational at least at the outset. However, the middle-class influx has been under way long enough for signs of permanence to be seen and fears therefore to diminish. The estates are spruce, the houses change hands far more rapidly than the older village houses, but when one of these does become available it goes, as often as not, to a technologist who has decided to stay. Intermarriage between the old and the new families is now frequent, and the great benefit of the invasion is that Sedgefield is now a relatively young village and thus has avoided that vicious circle in which an ageing population set their faces against new ideas and thus become more than ever entrenched in their ways. By contrast Sedgefield, because of its own primary schools and because it is the site for the district comprehensive, is each day the host to more than 1,000 children, and its social involvement is now heavily slanted towards the young. Thus is could cautiously be said to have the best of all possible worlds. It is ironical, when you think of it, that a village that erupted so ominously in my childish mind, should now be seen for the happy place it undoubtedly is. The old dames whispering furtively at the street corner ought to have another incarnation and see it as it is today.

14

Favourite Pubs

I HAVE travelled a few thousand miles all over Durham during the last year and had some hard words to say and harder thoughts unuttered about the pubs. The trouble is that I have felt a lack of welcome, a service which is extremely limited and an absence of atmosphere which has been consistent and at times pathetic. It is my experience which obviously is now widespread that you cannot drop in casually to a pub in too many of the villages of Durham and expect the enjoyment and relaxation you get almost everywhere in the villages in the South. I have long pondered why this is so, and before I ever embarked on the detailed scrutiny of a county this book has entailed, I received the same impression somewhat more fleetingly, not only in Durham but also in Northumberland. There, the fact that the village pub often situated in the most delectable spot is frequently enough without any pretension to charm or any of the qualities which might persuade the traveller to return, comes as even more of surprise. Because Northumberland is more of a rural county and not, as is Durham, the amalgam of the rural and the urban with the hint of industry always on the most beautiful horizons. In Durham, therefore, you may expect the workaday pub, the drinking place, serving a small and unpretentious community and that, perhaps too often, is what you get. In Northumberland the disappointment is more acute when, for example, you penetrate the villages in the valleys of the Coquet or the Tyne and find only the forgettable: have your refreshment quickly and pass on your way.

There are some honourable exceptions, sometimes in the most unlikely places. In Durham the same is true, only more rarely, and though I was eternally optimistic, hoping that the next village or hamlet would contain the jewel that would restore my faith in the virtues of North-country hospitality and the imagination with which it is purveyed, the optimism at times grew somewhat desperate.

What is wrong with the pubs? Well, first there is the beer. I happen not to like the caramel effusions you get in the majority of tied houses, and even in these places, by a marketing process which defeats me, you often enough get some of the brewery's beers—but not those which, by experienced judgement, are the best. Thus at the time of my pub survey and, indeed, during all the months of my Durham travels, there was an intense advertising campaign aiming at popularizing a bland, rather thin beer, served cold, and which, one suspects, was proving enjoyable to women. Eminent sportsmen were shown apparently as devotees of this brew (though one to my personal knowledge never touches the stuff). I doubt if it was an accident that every village pub I encountered which this brewery owned sold this beer and scarcely any, particularly the smaller ones, the one brew that takes my fancy. You seem to get less of this in the South, and certainly you are offered more of the local brews which, sadly, no longer exist in Durham. At many of the pubs, therefore, you have to take it or leave it, and though the choice is far wider at the diminishing number of free houses, the labels may be different, but the taste is usually approximately the same. There is, of course, a good deal of agitation for the barrel instead of the keg which is now in almost universal use, but this is ignored by the big brewers. I found only one pub in one village (Birtley) where the barrels have come back as a deliberate act of policy. It was significant that trade had increased, and customers were coming from a much wider area. The two other criticisms it seems to me reasonable to make about the average Durham village pub is on the score of comfort and what they offer you to eat. The only reason for optimism here is that though we are well behind the rest of the country in these respects, and especially the South, we are improving at a quite prodigious rate.

Ten years ago the situation would have been profoundly worse. I remember writing a series of articles about the state of the pub about 1960 and finding a considerable resistance at many of them to providing food at all.

Fly-blown sandwiches curling at the edges were reluctantly offered, and there was nothing between this and the institutional hotel and the set dining-room meal at rigid times. Instances multiplied at this time of inns refusing food and thereby contravening their legal obligation which was to purvey refreshments—in the broadest sense—to the traveller. I do not exaggerate and I do not believe that there is much controversy about the matter. The fact that we were so very far behind the rest of the country seemed to stem from attitudes more common with Scotland than the rest of England. It is a fair generalization that in Scotland pubs were (and still are) regarded as solemn drinking places where the frivolities of food and comfort were discounted—if they were considered at all. The puritan tradition which argued that comfortless hostelries would deter many from visiting them is strong. Perhaps the same force active in so many Durham villages through the old time Methodist church was a contributory cause at least to the barren, soul-less and downright forbidding nature of the public houses.

I am not of course suggesting that the situation is as bad today or that Methodism is as dominating as it was—only that this attitude is by no means gone, and as a result it is a highly chancey business to say the least to drop in on a Durham pub. I was never actually refused sustenance though at one it was indelicately suggested that nuts and potato crisps were adequate. Elsewhere hospitality was sometimes rough and ready and calculated to blunt all except the rudest appetite. So far as comfort was concerned, this was geared, in many instances, to a small, undemanding local custom. I suppose the offending pubs would argue that critical travellers are an infinitesimal part of their custom and that they cannot engage in extravagant provision for the sake of a few. What use providing tasty bar snacks at noon if the local and inviolable habit is to eat 'dinner' at home?

In reply to all this there is, happily, an increasing number of instances of village pubs imaginatively and on an appropriately limited scale, emerging as true centres for the community and havens of call for the traveller. They are finding that despite their isolation or workaday surroundings the customers are finding them out.

In this they are merely reflecting a more dramatic change which has taken place in the towns of Durham and in the city of Durham over the past decade in which lunch in the canteen or the corner café, or the sandwich in the office has been succeeded by what is known euphemistically as a pie and a pint at the local.

This explosion in lunch-time conviviality has been accompanied by the takeover of the local by women. How much this is in response to the marketing strategy of the brewers who simply and hardheadedly want to sell more of their products, and how much to domestic revolution is difficult to judge. Probably the first encouraged and speeded the momentum of the second. The effect has been to feminize and soften these previously male strongholds, and though this characteristic may have been common enough long enough in the South, its advent in Durham is relatively new and still far from being accepted in total. The whole situation, in any case, was complicated by the dominance in so many villages (and not necessarily colliery villages) of the working men's club which has been written about in some detail in another chapter. The point worth making here, though, is that women also invaded the club, which in its turn became more welcoming, and more truly a centre for the community. Where in the village the pubs have been brightened, and where they set themselves to provide a communal service is in response, often enough, to the competition the clubs invoked. Where this has not happened and, as I have made clear, this is still in the majority of places, it seems to be for a variety of causes.

First there is lack of will: the pub may be deemed cautiously by the brewery which owns it to be doing well enough and any process of revivification may either not be worth the capital expended or may siphon trade away from another of the brewery houses not far away. Then there is lack of aptitude. I could quote a dozen instances where pub-brightening attempts have failed so that they have become worse than before the brightening process began. This has happened because either the manager or tenant has no talent in this direction and lacks the essential imagination of the true host, or else senior management at the brewery, aware as it must be of this situation, does not have the energy or skill to make the requisite changes. There is the fear of management in attracting the wrong sort of custom, and this is especially true in essentially working-class villages where, it is felt, the tried and trusted all-the-year-round trade may disappear if attempts were made to attract the middle-class travellers in the summer by the imposition of such sophistications as fitted carpets and scampi and chips. There is finally the widespread belief that many of the villages do not have the trade, either actual or potential, and that tourism and domestic revolution notwithstanding, the welcome sign need not be hung out there. I hope to demonstrate how this can be proved to be untrue by citing one or two decidedly unpromising places where pubs have prospered exceedingly.

Pubs I did not like gave me sandwiches with thick bread and thin meat or had the pretension of the toasted sandwich with scarcely anything inside it at all. Counters were sometimes awash with beer and (a cardinal sin) glasses piled upon the tables, and ashtrays overflowed with the sleazy remnants of bags of potato crisps. Juke-boxes blared, this imposition on the rest of the clientèle being imposed without interference by a couple of teenagers. There was a perpetual shortage of ice, the lack of any cooling place for bottles and an air of suspicion because I, by accent, and diffident demands, betrayed the fact that I really belonged somewhere else.

Bar assistants while not precisely being rude, conveyed the air of preferring to do anything but grant my wishes, and the manager (in the single instance where I summoned him) would eminently have qualified for the old army charge of dumb insolence. From all this I would hate it to be inferred that the villages of Durham are full of bleak, unwelcoming hostelries; most are simply neutral, being neither one thing or the other and content in their limitations where (I maintain) they should not be. But, of course, I have had my infinite pleasures in pub hunting in Durham, and these pleasures have been the greatest where they have been the most surprising. I made a list of twenty or thirty pubs I thought pretty good, and narrowed it down to a dozen I adjudged excellent in every way. I have labelled them my dozen best pubs. The choice is idiosyncratic and readers of like mind will no doubt be able to provide their own list. Mine are in no particular order of merit and have only one virtue in common: they inspired in me a determination to return and to spread the glad tidings of their existance wherever I went.

The New Inn is on a high and advantageous promontory at Iveston, a village we have not visited before though the area is familiar enough. The A691 wends its rolling way from Gateshead. One turns off this road at Leadgate in the Durham direction and Iveston is on the hinterland a mile or two away. The village is ancient and pushes in linear fashion in the direction of Annfield Plain being surrounded nowadays by the moors of North-west Durham. It had a booming nineteenth-century prosperity when coal and iron was worked. All this has long gone. A few of the old houses have been adapted; a few vast new bungalows have been built and the village with its Anglo Saxon grassy swards is a pleasant haven for the well-to-do. Once you recover from the surprise of seeing the inn there at all you realize how beautifully it is situated. Everything is rural apart from the omnipresent smoke from the chimneys of Consett on the western horizon.

The first (and only) snag I encountered was the large alsatian lying sprawled across the main entrance to the pub. Though my sense told me that it must be harmless I have a pathological mistrust of this breed and might even have avoided this place at all. Fortunately I found a side entrance.

Inside this free house there were seven or eight draught beverages on offer including that rarity in the North, draught cider. It was all beautifully clean, and though refurbishing had recently been carried out there was nothing offensively 'twee' in the decor. Though the 'old' ceiling beams were made yesterday, no attempt was made to indicate otherwise. Bar snacks were diverse and imaginative; there was an infinite variety of sandwiches and the dining room almost the place for a gourmet. The staff smiled; even the alsatian, by now indoors, proved as idiotically friendly as I had hoped.

At Annfield Plain, not so far away, but reached by a curious conglomeration of minor roads through Stony Heap and East Castle, the presence of another inn of real distinction is even more remarkable. Annfield Plain is squarely in the centre of Category D territory—that depressed area of North-west Durham previously referred to in which the pits are dead, the communities perhaps decaying, and villages are permitted by official edict to die. Annfield itself carries the usual evidence of pitmatic prosperity of long ago, but its single colliery is now used for training purposes. It is in no sense an insult to Annfield Plain to suggest that nobody need go there: no one from the towns of Consett and Stanley, moving to Newcastle, Durham or to the Motorway, has cause to pass through Annfield Plain which, in any case, is accomplished in a moment. There is nothing picturesque or historical about Annfield Plain. Fordyce, that frequently quoted (by me) and sometimes verbose historian can write only seven lines about Annfield Plain, yet here is situated 'The Plainsman', supporting the theory that it is almost irrelevant where a good pub is to be found since news of its happy existence spreads quickly among the perceptive travellers.

When I was there, a straw poll revealed customers from Newcastle, Sunderland, Durham, a flurry of locals, and a single holiday-maker from Norway. There are the usual spurious beams, copper-topped tables and little red lamps, but the atmosphere exudes friendliness and the mince and two dumplings (being eaten in a heat wave), as well as the less sustaining fare were spoiled only by the permeation of pop music which suddenly assailed the room. This is another free house and its triumph, it seems to me, is in becoming an acknowledged haven for local drinkers, and the target for the relatively distant traveller who likes good food—especially unpretentious but excellent home cooking.

'The Biddick' at Fatfield is beside the occasionally odiferous river Wear and equidistant from Washington Old Hall and the Penshaw Monument, both of which we have previously encountered. There is not, at first sight, any reason for its growing reputation, for the beer, dispensed from the keg and coming exclusively from a giant brewery combine, is without particular distinction. 'The Biddick' gains by comparison with the arid—indeed almost non-existent—nature of the hospitality dispensed in the neighbourhood, but this would not be sufficient in itself to bring people, almost in hordes from the nearby Washington New Town, this clientèle including company executives with expense accounts which would cover bills far in excess of anything they are liable to incur at 'The Biddick'. The reputation, built up quietly over a period is for home-cooked food at reasonable cost—the type of menu no expense account may demand at an institutional hotel. The luncheon room is full of amiable clutter; brass and copper plates, reproductions of *The Laughing Cavalier* and the *Mona Lisa*, swords, pistols and miners' lamps, while climbing plants positively drip from the ceiling. But no matter, the stock-pot soup is a feast in itself, and the braised steak and onions just as I dimly recall my mother making it. Service can get somewhat neurotic at peak times, but on the whole the operation revolves efficiently round a landlord who has perceived that homely food is the crying need.

The implication at 'The Biddick' which happy customers find so alluring is that if you want a quick and expensive grill you must go somewhere else.

'The Red Lion' at West Boldon is quite different from those previously mentioned in that it has no pretensions towards special food and offers only sandwiches and the occasional meal in a basket. This whitewashed pub was kept during my several visits by two women, mother and daughter, kindly martinets for whom 'standards' are crucial. It is right beside the A184 and can become mightily mudsplashed on occasion. At one time the ladies used to be escorted by three dogs which added to the personality of the place. They were Fred, a Doberman, and a couple of lesser lights named Henry and Bunty. The place is full of antiques, the acquisition of which is a great love in the life of Etta, the tenant. Various annexes have names like The Tudor Room and The Board Room, and there are stained-glass windows announcing that after toil comes rest. The place is brewery tied and without what I consider to be the best beer that brewery makes. A slight suggestion of coyness is soon forgotten, and the place's character comes from the astringence of the hostesses. I doubt if they suffer fools gladly but they do cherish their friends. Conversation ranges widely, is radical by inclination though strictly non-political, but is likely to take in abortion, the economy, the telly and the sins and omissions of Sunderland Football Club whose ground can be reached in a few minutes by fast car. A few indigenous countrymen foregather, as does the occasional miner from Boldon Colliery down the bank. 'The Red Lion' thus becomes the utterly unself-conscious melting pot of the classes—just as a good pub should be.

'The Britannia' on the corner of the A19 and the village street at Cleadon has a continuing village public house tradition but nowadays the modern and, to some extent, packaged look one of the main brewery combines is giving to their out-of-town pubs. It was a staging point on the turnpike road from South Shields, and there was a pot house on the site before the days of the stage coach. Old prints of Cleadon village at the turn of this century show a far more modest 'Britannia' in the middle of the few houses and the pond which then comprised the village.

The refurbishing of a decade or so ago was aimed at capitalizing on the fact that Cleadon was no longer a village in its original isolated sense but had large executive appendages. The place was greatly increased in size and whereas the bar was left more or less in its original and proletarian state, the lounge, done entirely in rural brick, even had gold fish in a pond. A dining-room annexe was grafted on the end. This was the fashion of several other pubs owned by this combine in Durham and Northumberland. I have patronized most of them and think 'The Britannia' is the best since it avoids the coy and pretentious atmosphere gold-fish thinking generates, while its restaurant, though avowedly a simple grill room, is unflurried and with charming attention at even the times of peak demand. It has also skilfully avoided any deterioration in its clientèle which is no easy matter when football supporters pass the door. On crowded evenings there is a sort of glowering middle-class resentment if—on the rare occasions—the lounge is penetrated by a peripatetic yobbo element. But they, being denied juke box, fruit machine, and the company of their kind, have no answer to the united disapproval of the regulars and quickly go away. Unlike 'The Red Lion', you cannot easily become involved in the general conversation, 'The Britannia' being a pleasant place at which you arrive—and depart—with your friends.

Miles away on the moors above Lanchester is the Punch Bowl Inn at Satley. This is controlled by the same brewery as 'The Britannia', but has developed somewhat differently since whereas the vicinity of 'The Britannia' is urban and densely populated, 'The Punch Bowl' is in the middle of nowhere. Still, as I have mentioned, the traveller emerging from isolation usually courts disappointment at the wayside inn in Durham. Not so at 'The Punch Bowl'. I have penetrated the mists at Lanchester on a November midday and the snows of January and been mightily glad for the smiles, the efficient service, the well-grilled steak. The chief virtue of 'The Punch Bowl' is not that it is so very marvellous but that, considering the isolation, it is there at all.

Like 'The Biddick', 'The Ravensworth Arms' derives a large custom from industry—in its case from the factories and offices of the Team Valley Trading Estate a mile or so away. They come usually in the middle of the day for bar snacks of a quite astonishing cheapness. 'The Ravensworth' is marvellously sited in a tundra of isolation among, but not part of, the old colliery villages of Lamesley and Kibblesworth, and stretching as far as further hamlets of a like nature at Ouston, Urpeth and Perkinsville. Within this territory the club reigns almost without opposition, and a drive of twenty miles round the byways that seem to point to nowhere, comes across no place where the flag of hospitality may be said to be flying. That is, of course, with the exception of 'The Ravensworth' which also has an enviable business as an evening centre for dinner parties. They have a booking system; dinner is twice nightly and the main attraction is the gratifying sense that however grand the menu, the bill is never quite as much as you have feared.

The two pubs in the delightful village of Elwick deserve mentioning in any guide to popular boozers in Durham, though if I lived there I would be inclined to curse the fascination they undoubtedly exert. Elwick, in the days before motorways and fast cars must have been remote indeed and largely undiscovered by the traveller, for though it is less than a mile from the A19 as this near-motorway moves within sight of the ICI colossus at Billingham, it belongs securely to the world of the minor road. The village has considerable antiquity and includes the typical Anglo Saxon green. Five of its inhabitants took part in that Rising of the North against Queen Elizabeth in 1569 and one was executed. It is only in the last couple of decades, though, that the village has been discovered in the modern sense with some fine new houses as one

approaches the old village, and more of the same in a cul-de-sac in
the village centre. All this is splendid and you can recline beneath
a giant sycamore in the centre of the green and reflect how pleasant
it would be to own one of the few early Victorian houses within
your gaze. But you have to reckon with being submerged by the
motor car every fine weekend, this being due more to the lure of
'The McOrville' and 'The Spotted Cow', two splendidly contrast-
ing village pubs within a couple of doors of each other, than to
any of the undoubted rural delights.

'The McOrville', named after a famous but now forgotten
Victorian racehorse trained in the vicinity, is the very epitome of
friendliness. When the English exile, thousands of miles from
home in a climate that bakes or freezes talks of his yearning for
the 'typical' village pub, I imagine he must have 'The McOrville'
in the front of his mind. There is a small bar at which people talk
animatedly and without much heed as to whether they know you
or not. Subjects: football—it is only a few miles from the ground
of the resurgent Middlesbrough team—politics, radical by almost
unanimous consent, but no party affiliations discernible.

Gossip of the village including the prices luxury new houses
are fetching just along the road. Holiday tragedies, including how
we were double booked in Majorca. Natural history: unanimous
support for foxhunting. All this before lunch on a weekday while
the bar speedily fills, for lunch is another of the lures (aside from
'The McOrville's' unpretentious charm) that brings people out
from the grabbing money-making cosmopolitanism of Teesside.
Here the steaks are always tender, the hot pot a dream, the salads
artistically as well as comestibly perfect. Everything is home
cooked, home supervised, home tasting—really super. Eight small
tables all crowded together, and a theory in action by the homely
management. "If you make it good, people will roll up." So they
do.

'The Spotted Cow', which is grander and bigger, is altogether
more 'pop' with a rack of wine on prominent display, Perry Como
wailing (though as if from a distance) on the muted public-address
system, and an air of brisk efficiency. The food is perhaps more
predictable, and personally I would choose 'The McOrville' every
time. But hundreds of people do not. The village, as I said, seethes
with the motor car: the penalty it must continue to pay for being
near enough unique in having a couple of pubs that are a positive
pleasure.

This emotion is also aroused by 'The Seven Stars' at Shincliffe.

We have seen in another chapter that the village has a distinguished amalgam of residents and this is reflected in 'The Seven
Stars' customers. Academics, planners, students, newspaper editors,
two very rich people, a market gardener and a couple of building
site workers unite in appreciation of an atmosphere somewhat akin
to that at 'The Red Lion' at Boldon, but may be more challenging,
since the spread of human experience is a bit wider. There is also
a lot of interesting impedimenta; a massive snake skin pinned to
the ceiling, china dogs on the mantleshelf and pit lamps everywhere. The tenant does not serve; she mingles, encouraging the
family atmosphere that brings people several miles (and past a
number of pubs) just to luxuriate in what the others have not got.

'The Three Tuns' at Birtley deserves inclusion. There is nothing
salubrious about its surroundings (it is by the side of the noisy,
lorry-ridden road castigated in another chapter) but is cool in a
heat wave, and has beer from the wood. This is a place, tied to a
relatively small Yorkshire brewery, where most of the kegs have
been taken out and barrels reintroduced in response to popular
demand. Discerning beer drinkers should find this place worth a
detour—and the management is friendly.

'The Rose and Crown' at Romaldskirk has been touched on in
the chapter on Teesdale, and is worth a visit for its rural charm,
though one has to be careful of the beer—from another small
Yorkshire brewery which is marvellous but unusually potent. Twice
recommended, though, if you happen to be staying the night.
Otherwise sip sparingly and derive your inspiration from the conversation which is far reaching, unacademic, and nicely lacking in
abstractions. Finally, 'The Pot and Glass' at Egglescliffe is completely the rural pub in this most rural of all Durham villages. Beer
unexceptional, but locals and car trade blend nicely together.

15

Apologia

THERE was this problem, you see, as to whether Tyne Dock with its decaying railway arches, and faintly disreputable urban air truly was a village. Indisputably Tyne Dock was the place where long ago you took a tram to the sea for a penny, it was a sort of junction between places (Jarrow and South Shields) which incontestably were towns. But a village?

Then there was East Jarrow, once isolated in greenery, near the church of Bede, near the Tyne, a place of vivid character for me, largely owing to my father's eloquence. But now, you blink as you speed along the road beside the trading estate and East Jarrow is gone. It is questionable, whether, indeed, it exists at all. Yet my grandfather, bearded Victorian that he was, found the lighted cottage windows there a beacon as he trudged over the snow from Sunderland. East Jarrow was as enclosed an entity and as separate from its surroundings as any metropolis. Now it lingers, the few brown stones of it on the outskirts of a trading estate, and Jarrow, East Jarrow, Tyne Dock and South Shields are one sprawl or blur on the banks of the Tyne, the villages that were merged with the towns that are so that it is impossible to distinguish one from the other.

This last chapter is an apologia, in its way, for barely mentioned places and those I have missed all together. It is a continuance of the theme tentatively explored in the previous chapter, but an extension, too. For there are places in Durham County which defy categorization. They were villages before the Industrial Revolution, before the shipyards appeared on the river banks, before collieries and colliery dwellings linked them one with the other. For then, as my grandfather was never tired of reminding the small boy who sat at the table with him on winter nights, and listened by the light of the oil lamps to his rolling reminiscence, then there were stretches of dark and silent country always between one ham-

M

let and the other. His grandfather had told him how in the 1830s if you took your girl down the Lonnen which stretched from Jarrow to Hedworth, your best friend took his girl and strolled just behind.

Each of you grasped a stout stick, for the footpads lurked in among the hawthorn and the deadly nightshade, and once in a while some one got a cracked head and lost the only shilling he possessed.

Ah, well, Hedworth was a village then; not idealized, but earthy, with a pond and rickety cottages, swarms of children who died young, and a public house where the cheap gin was a curse. Still Hedworth would have qualified even fifty years ago, but they built council houses all over the Lonnen so that between the wars nomads returning to the places of their youth became utterly confounded. And subsequently they have so interspersed the green fields towards Boldon Colliery with motorways, that the quiet land behind the Greyhound Inn has been lost, and Brockley Whins, a hamlet that arose from the dawn of the railway age has disappeared forever. But what of Boldon Colliery? A colliery village like all the others? In many superficial ways this is true. But you arouse the ire of its proud inhabitants if you airily come to this conclusion. Boldon Colliery is not beautiful but it has tradition and attainment and distinguished sons: Lord Lawson who became Minister of War in a Labour Government and Sam Waton a shrewd moderate miners' secretary. It also has the archetypal pit cottages, modernized, cosy and warm, now being preserved by the planners. Once you could have pulled them down overnight and no one would have cared; now they are seen as enviable citadels of the past, stately homes of the common people.

But then the choice of colliery villages had to be arbitrary; one had to risk the anger of people like those in Boldon who felt that they were special—as indeed they all were. For how do you distinguish between the excellences of the people of Langley Park which I visited—and Metal Bridge and Boldon, which I did not. In Metal Bridge, if I had cared to delve, a vivid recent, teeming life would have been uncovered. I have heard tales of the village cricket match there which would outdo any ever told by Mary Russell Mitford, and I have heard grown men speak with nostalgic affection of the closed, cosy, incredibly contained life lived there. A book could be written about Metal Bridge alone; a book should be.

Then there was Hetton, Hylton, Herrington, Pelton, Plawsworth,

Murton, Trimdon, Fishburn, Lumley, pit villages all, each united by a shared experience, each separated by subtle differences. To the outsider perhaps from the South they all seem incredibly alike: long rows of colliery cottages: old pitmen in the clubs, reminiscing eternally of the days of purpose when small pits made money, men bathed by the fireside, and the clogs on the cobbles as men rushed to the first shift roused small children from their slumbers.

You see the sameness; you have to ferret out the differences. Books, truly could be written about each and every village in which the winding engine gear, now silent at the quiet pithead, is the modern monument to vanished days. You could fill an encyclopaedia, as large as Fordyce's *History of Durham*, with the social history of the pit villages of Durham as heard from the mouths of the people. Perhaps we should do this before it is too late, recording the differing attitudes of Metal Bridge on one side of the vast spoil heap, and Cornforth on the other, and explaining why they think one way in Easington (which I visited) and somewhat differently in Horden and Blackhall (which I did not).

But of course, doing this, you would come up against the old problem I have had to face everywhere for a year. Are they villages any longer? For as they have spread outwards and council estates have been grafted upon them, as petrol stations, bus stops, warehouses, occasional small factories have burgeoned along the roads that used to be winding rural arteries, village has merged into village, and only the signposts at the roadside enable the traveller without acute local knowledge to determine where he may be.

The merger may also be given impetus in the benighted name of local government efficiency. Re-organization—the dreaded word —imposes a crass uniformity as I have indicated more than once elsewhere. Surprisingly, though, amid all this clamour, many of the people retain an intense feeling for place, so that it still becomes heinous to confuse South Hetton with Hetton le Hole, or not to appreciate the significant dividing line between Framwellgate Moor and Pity Me.

Local pride finds other expressions. Everywhere I went as I insinuated myself down the county's coastline with frequent forays inland, I came across monster graffiti announcing "The Murton Boys Have Been Here". One such banner, in letters two feet high, was emblazoned on an old viaduct; merely to reach the place must have required the ingenuity and staff work of a military operation. This, and all the other similar examples of this village's public relations were not more than three miles from Murton itself proving, I suppose, that there was still a feeling of close identity with a place which long since has been submerged in an amorphous urban tentacle. The boys who achieved this sort of immortality (for the graffiti will last as long as the viaduct and this, being Victorian, is now a building of special distinction) were not hooligan in intention. I tracked them down, discovering shy and inarticulate bewilderment, aggression only being displayed when defending the merits of the dark streets of Murton, and the fascinations and waywardness of the Sunderland Football Club.

I have written of the villages that used to be on the banks of the industrial Tyne, but there are others omitted for which apology should be made. Heworth, for instance, with a church which, with the green fields ahead, used to be the beginning of adventure. Now it is at the end of a by-pass from Newcastle with lorries churning round the roundabout and a pub, far from any cricket field, inconsequentially called 'The Maiden Over'. Further down there is Pelaw of which I know nothing. Even Fordyce has little to say of Pelaw— or Pelaw Main—except that it was a hamlet which housed a public house and a boat builders' shop. Pelaw is fixed in my mind as being a place where they manufactured polish and where an aunt's war work in 1914–18 was to make shirts. A fading photograph, before me as I write, is of this aunt wearing one of the shirts or blouses she made, sitting in a high Victorian sewing chair, bent studiously at some industrious task with wool.

I have mentioned some of the villages now part of greater Sunderland and indistinguishable from the rest of it. But I haven't mentioned Southwick, high above a bridge over the Wear, still known as 'the village' by the inhabitants, still, in its quieter moments, having the air of the eighteenth century, but for most of the time submerged utterly in the fumes and cacophony of the present. East Herrington is the same; Middle Herrington slightly less so. Both were quiet retreats separated from the considerable county borough of Sunderland by a few miles of rolling countryside. Now—and insidiously since the war—the miles have been eaten up by council estates. The same is true of Grindon where there used to be only a pub, a few houses and acres of nothing. I am not saying this is a doleful story, but it is a true one whereever in the county you go.

I missed Cockfield, despite the urgings of the Rector of Middleton, but with respect, the strangest stories of this former colliery village just north of the Tees are in the past—and none stranger, anywhere, than that of Jeremiah Dixon, son of a servant at Raby

Castle, a self-educated genius whose expertise is said to have included mathematics, mineralogy, chemistry and hydraulics. In such great esteem was he held in the middle eighteenth century that he was chosen by the Royal Academy at Woolwich to be sent to St Helena to observe the transit of Venus across the sun. Undergoing his scrutiny for this task he was asked: "Where did you study mathematics, at Oxford or Cambridge—and which public school did you attend?" He denied the first question and answered the second thus: "At no public school, sirs, but in a pit cabin at Cockfield Fell." He is credited at least with the joint discovery of coal gas with the roughest of apparatus, his retort consisting of an old tea kettle. He was buried in an old chapel at Raby but this was pulled down by one of the Dukes of Cleveland and a dog kennel built on the site. He is undoubtedly the most famous of the sons of this small village and one of the most remarkable people the county has ever produced.

Where else did I miss? An infinite variety of hamlets so miniscule that they ought not to have names, but did.

Places off the A19? I must have visited a score but there were twenty or thirty more tiny places with just a house or two and a name. Hamlets galore in the great plain around Sedgefield, and also, Wynyard.

Wynyard seems a place all right, for there is a name by the side of the road near Thorpe Thewles and Wolviston and all within sight, virtually, of those steaming towers of Teesside. But Wynyard, well, it is nothing but a big house, and I would set my face and mind against big houses and castles, not to mention churches. At least in theory I did because they have all been written about too much before in that formalistic dull way, and unless a church is like Escomb which thrills me by its mystery, or a castle is like Raby or Brancepeth which naturally fitted into my peregrinations, I am sorry, but I did not want to know. But Wynyard, well, this was a bit different, too, since, I had been there already, and been shown round fifteen years ago by the very young Lord Londonderry, and it was not only remarkable for its history, but fitting snugly into contemporary life as well.

The Londonderrys, of course, proliferated all over east Durham, powerful industrial monarchs, and Wynyard was the scene of probably the most dramatic and costly fire in the county in the nineteenth century. In 1822 an ancient mansion on the site was razed to the ground and the building commenced of a magnificent mansion in the Grecian style. On the night of 19th February 1841, this mansion, when nearly complete was burnt to the ground in a conflagration that suffused the whole countryside in a hectic rosy glow. The damage was conservatively estimated at £150,000 and it would be interesting to know how many millions that would mean today. Valuable pictures were destroyed; so was an exotic conservatory filled with rare plants; so were superb mantleshelves worth £1,000 each. The present mansion is as faithful a copy of that which was lost as could be achieved, and it has resounded, in latter years, to fine music and dancing since the châtelaine, the present Lady Londonderry, is a ballet dancer of international renown.

I drove out of the gates of Wynyard, pointed the car north, and ended up, in due time, back in the village of Monkton where this journey began. Things were approximately the same in Monkton, the rubble of the slag-heap being as omnipresent as ever, though a few thousand tons had undoubtedly been whittled away since I had last gazed upon it. The Church of the Venerable Bede, dismal and empty at the book's beginning, was now in process of demolition—so time had marched on. I tried to think which was the finest village I had visited and concluded that comparisons were certainly invidious. I did not think that the people were finer than in other parts, either, though they were quirky and quixotic and forthright, and I did not reckon you would ever dictate to them, politically or otherwise. I think if you are looking for constant picturesqueness you had better go elsewhere, but Durham, my county, has got the dignity I cherish.

Postscript

As proofs of this book arrived, approximately eighteen months after I made the first Durham journey and wrote the first word, I decided to rush round some of the key villages again.

Little of significance had changed, but in Westoe (see Chapter two) they have now imposed the yellow lines they tried so hard to resist, and therefore spirited the intrusive cars away.

They also now prevent direct access to the A19, making the village even more of a cocoon. My general argument about the village seems as valid as ever.

One other final point, which is simply a slight apology for using 'pitmatic' several times—a word of the Northern vernacular which decidedly is in no dictionary. I cannot think, though, that the word is in any danger of being misunderstood.

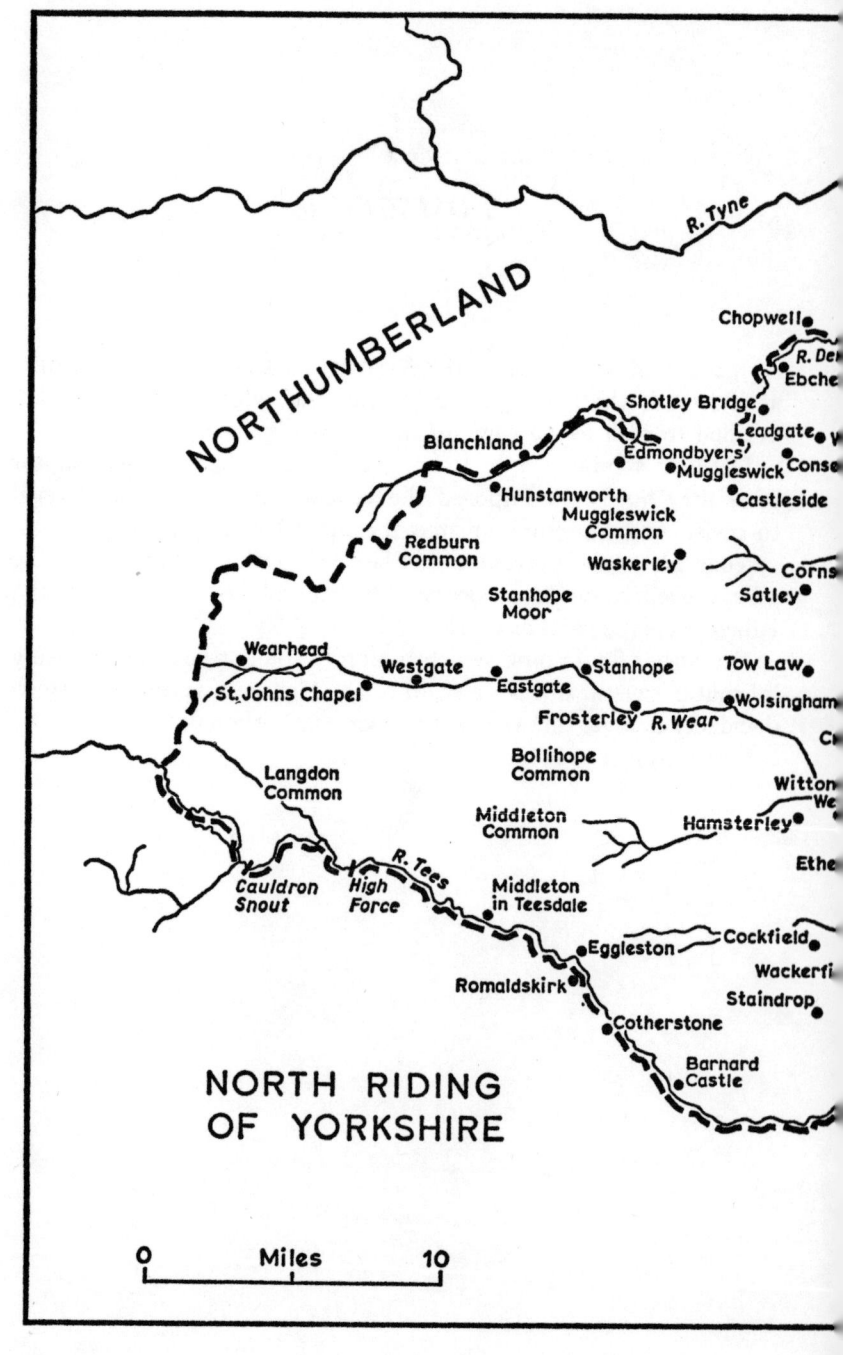

NORTH RIDING
OF YORKSHIRE

Index